The Power of a Positive Mindset

The Power of a Positive Mindset

TRANSFORM YOUR MIND TRANSFORM YOUR LIFE

By

Jason Wolbers

ISBN: 979-8-9885343-0-3 (paperback)
ISBN: 979-8-9885343-1-0 (hardback)
ISBN: 979-8-9885343-2-7 (ebook)

Introduction

I started my career as a professional salesperson selling in-home fire-safety-related products fresh out of high school. I was eighteen years old. I still joke with my parents today about how college would have wasted my time and their money as I wasn't interested in a college degree. I was, however, very interested in furthering my education. From the day I started in sales, I made it my job not only to learn as much as I could about the company and products I was selling, but I spent equal time learning about people and motivation! I wanted to know what motivated people to buy our products and also learn how to motivate myself and others to maintain high enthusiasm. I wanted to inspire people. My sales career was successful, and I was near the top of the sales leaderboards nationally every week, month, and year. In this book I share the motivational information I learned in my sales career. I hope you find it helpful as I did.

At twenty-three I decided to branch off the dealership I had worked in for five and a half years *(working for my parents)* and moved to a new state to start my own office with the same parent company. *(That's the normal progression in the business we are in.)* I was in for a rude awakening. I had mastered the art of sales and motivation but needed to learn more about running my own business. My wife, Tara, and I were in for the ride of our lives. In the following pages, I'll teach you many things I had to learn to get through this phase of my life and career. These were the tough/broke years of my life, but I continued to learn new things and ways to stay motivated.

We took that leap into running our own business in January 2001 with little to no business sense. I was very good at sales, and Tara was very good at marketing, but we needed to improve in almost every other area. Now for the rest of the story, we are still in the same business and have succeeded after the first few years of barely getting by! How did we figure it all out? How did we get better in all of the areas we were weak? How did we become one of the top offices in our business year after year? This book contains what we learned during this challenging season, and we learned a ton. We had no choice; it was either learn and get better or be bankrupt and start all over. You'd understand the latter wasn't an option if you knew me. We were determined to keep learning and improving, and we did just that!

We were always willing to learn new things; we went all over the United States to meetings and seminars, stayed plugged into all company events, and promoted the opportunity to help build the company every day of our lives. WE WERE ALL IN! We made it our responsibility to not only learn everything we could about running a successful business, but then to pay it forward and teach as many people those same principles we were learning along the way. WE NEVER GAVE UP; there were times when we probably should've! This book will give you practical ways to keep going when the going gets tough; our going got very tough at times, but by using the principles you'll learn in the next ninety days of reading this book, we persevered and became very successful. Want the best news? YOU CAN BE TOO. I believe wholeheartedly in this quote by Napoleon Hill, *"Whatever the mind of a man can conceive and believe, it CAN achieve."*

YOU, yes, I said YOU, can live your dreams. Just stay the course over the next ninety days, and take each page of this book to heart. I certainly had YOU in mind each day when I wrote it. You'll have days when it's hard to squeeze this reading in, when you're too tired, busy, don't feel well, on vacation, and many other distractions. I had those days while writing the book too. Taking a day off is ok, but get back at it the next day and keep reading daily. I wrote this hoping you would read it ninety days straight to build momentum in your life, so do your best to read every day. I sincerely hope that the principles and daily practices I teach in this book will help you achieve greatness in whatever area of your life you desire.

I may not be the most successful person to have ever written a book, but I am one of the most passionate people on the planet when it comes to helping others. I believe God put me on this earth to help people, and that's what my intention was when writing the book. I want you to be inspired and motivated when you read it daily.

In simple terms I hope you gain a new perspective on life *(a positive one)* over the next ninety days as you read each daily message, complete the **Today's Challenge**, read and recite the **Positive Affirmation of the Day** for each daily reading, and finally look at and think about each ***Quote of the Day*** at the end of every reading.

I sincerely hope you become better, happier, and more positive by reading this book. I hope you find new ways to rid yourself of bad habits and develop new positive habits to replace them. I want you to be inspired every time you pick up the book, read that day's writing, go out, and inspire others because of what you learned. With all of that in mind, I will ask you one favor. PAY IT FORWARD! Teach someone in your life all of the new things you learn from this book each day; then, by me writing it and you reading it, we can *"change the world, one person at a time"* and help you and the people around you to *"think more positive daily."*

Happy reading,
Jason Wolbers

Day One

Reset and Recharge

Every day is full of new opportunities. Today is no different! It's your first day of the ninety-day challenge to improve your life and mindset! It's also the first day of the rest of your life. Today is a great day to look back on life's accomplishments and the challenges that you've faced. Depending on how life has gone so far, we will all have a different perspective on what RESET may mean…

If you've had a good life, you're likely excited to continue building on that success! Just be sure you still have clearly defined goals moving forward, continue with the plans you already have set, and run full steam ahead! Those of you in this category, congrats, but remember that you have momentum right now, and your RESET may be to keep the momentum going. Keep setting new goals as you achieve the goals you're already working so hard for!

If you're looking back on life with regrets and goals that went unachieved, your RESET will look a lot different. The good news is that it's pretty simple if you fall into this category. Just take the time to set some new and exciting goals and develop a plan to achieve them moving forward! Doing so will be fun as it will help you forget past woes and give you something to look forward to tomorrow and beyond. This year could be your best if you plan for it and tell yourself daily it will be! So what are you waiting for? *RESET AND RECHARGE!*

Today's Challenge: If life has been great, reset by keeping the momentum going and continuing with the plans you're already successfully working on. If not reset by setting some new and exciting goals for this year and then take the time to develop a plan to achieve them.

Positive Affirmation of the Day: Today is the first day of the rest of my life, and I will live it to the fullest. (Do this in the mirror.)

Quote of the Day: "Every moment is a fresh beginning." —T.S. Eliot

Day Two

Positive Affirmations

YESTERDAY WE TALKED about resetting and recharging by setting some new goals. Today we will talk about calling those goals into existence through positive affirmations.

How we talk to ourselves is vital to our attitude, and our attitude is the most important asset any of us has! Zig Ziglar used to say, "A positive attitude won't help us to be able to do anything, but…it will help us do everything better." I agree with Zig 100%.

Today I want you to look at some of the goals you set for yourself yesterday and then go to the nearest mirror, look yourself right in the eye, and call it out in faith as if it has already happened (OUT LOUD). Yes, I'm asking you to look at yourself in the mirror and talk positively to yourself. It will be a little uncomfortable if you've never done it before, but you have to trust me on this one and go ahead and do it anyway because IT WORKS!!!

I want you to think about how good it feels when someone else says something positive to you or about you, and then I want you to ask yourself these questions: Do I say nice things to myself? Do I build myself up? Do I believe in myself? Doing positive daily affirmations will make you happier, help you appreciate what you already have in life, and make you eager to go after what you want but don't have yet!

Try it. You'll be glad you did.

Today's Challenge: Go back to yesterday's reading, get in front of a mirror, do that positive affirmation, and then do today's. Get used to talking good about yourself, and start doing this multiple times per day. (Warning. It will be uncomfortable at first, but do it anyway.)

Positive Affirmation of the Day: I will talk positively to myself from this day forward. I deserve good things in my life. (Do this in the mirror.)

Quote of the Day: "Accept yourself, and keep moving forward. If you want to fly, you have to give up what weighs you down." —Roy T. Bennett

We Become What We Think About

TODAY I WANT you to focus on your thoughts and consciously put some time into what you think about. We are doing this because, good or bad, our thoughts become things!

Think back to all the good and bad things that have happened in your life, and if you're 100% honest with yourself, you'll see this principle has already been at work in your life subconsciously! I'm asking you to make a conscious effort from today forward to think more about the things you do want to happen in your life rather than the things you don't want! Either way you'll be thinking them right into happening. So why not use this "secret" to your advantage and start living the life you want?

(CHANGE THE CHANNEL!)

I regularly use this exercise when I catch myself thinking negative thoughts. I immediately change the channel in my mind and think about something different that makes me positive and happy! What would you do if something came on TV that you didn't want to watch? That's right; you'd change the channel and watch something you like! That's all I'm asking you to do with your thoughts! We truly do become what we think about! What are you becoming?

Today's Challenge: Take some time to reflect on how your thoughts have affected the direction of your life positively and negatively because we've all had this happen both ways. Also practice the "change the channel" technique today when negative thoughts enter your mind…because they will. The difference now is you won't be dwelling on them, and you'll be changing the channel to something positive and moving on!

Positive Affirmation of the Day: I can and will think positively today! I'm in total control of my thoughts! I'm a positive thinker! (Do this in the mirror.)

Quote of the Day: "The positive thinker sees the invisible, feels the intangible, and achieves the impossible." —Winston Churchill

Day Four

PMA

PMA, or positive mental attitude, is one of the most significant assets any of us can have. The good news is that we can all develop this fantastic mentality. While there will undoubtedly be days and even seasons of our lives where we will struggle with keeping our heads up and staying positive, my experience has been that when you buy into a positive mindset and start developing better daily habits, you'll find that the days where you struggle with this will become fewer and far between.

Is it easy? No, but it's ALWAYS POSSIBLE! It's only day four of our mindset challenge, and we've already covered goals, positive affirmations, and control how we think (changing the mental channel). These are all habits we can work on every day. A positive outlook and attitude in life are 100% within our control. Learning and then applying the topics and exercises we will cover in the pages of this book will make developing and eventually maintaining a positive outlook and mindset in our lives much more accessible. A positive attitude comes naturally to some; however it has to be learned and practiced for most of us.

We will dig deeper and cover many positive habits in the coming days. For today I want to continue working on the things we've covered in the first few days. When we learn just how vital our attitude and mindset are to our overall joy and happiness, we become free to live the life of our dreams. So what are you waiting for? Start setting some goals (day one), talk positively to yourself (day two), take control of your thoughts (day three), and watch as your overall happiness starts to improve. It's invigorating when we begin to see the progress that occurs when we make a few positive changes in our lives and habits. Make some changes today!

Today's Challenge: Work on your goals a little more today, do a few positive affirmations, and continue to work on changing the mental channel in your mind when negative thoughts enter.

Positive Affirmation of the Day: I have a positive outlook in life, and I'm getting better every day. (Do this in the mirror.)

Quote of the Day: "Virtually nothing on earth can stop a person with a positive attitude who has his goal clearly in sight." —Dennis Waitley

DAY FIVE

Exercise

EXERCISE IS ONE of the best things we can do for our bodies and minds! Today let's consider the benefits of working out for us. It's obvious the effects exercise has on our body itself; it makes us look and feel better about ourselves, no doubt about it. But what does it do for our minds? That may be the more important thing to consider, considering we all already know what it does for our bodies.

A quick Google search on the subject helped me find this quote from HelpGuide.org, "Exercise can help provide: The same endorphins that make you feel better also help you concentrate and feel mentally sharp for tasks at hand. Exercise also stimulates the growth of new brain cells and helps prevent age-related decline."

Imagine how much more productive and positive our lives would be if we could feel more mentally sharp, create new brain cells regularly, and prevent age-related decline. All of us would sign up for those things for sure.

So today let's help ourselves and at least get out and take a short walk. You'll only know how something that simple will make you feel physically and mentally when you do it, and regular exercise will transform your self-image overnight. So what are you waiting for?

Today's Challenge: If you already have a regular exercise regimen, do that today as usual, but if you haven't been exercising, today's challenge will be simple and easy. Go for a short but brisk walk; walk as fast as possible while feeling comfortable. Walk for fifteen–thirty minutes, depending on how it feels. Afterward give yourself a pat on the back. JUST DO IT!

Positive Affirmation of the Day: *I* CAN AND WILL EXERCISE; I feel good physically and mentally! (Do this in the mirror.)

Quote of the Day: "The pain you feel today will be the strength you feel tomorrow." —Anonymous

DAY SIX

The Golden Rule

WE'VE ALL HEARD the old saying, "Do unto others as you would have them do unto you," right? This phrase is also known as the Golden Rule, and it's the single best rule of life any of us can ever learn. It also has a Bible verse to prove its truth. (See today's quote below.)

When we treat others with dignity and respect, we will almost always get that same dignity and respect back in return. You might say, "But some people don't reciprocate the same kindness I show them." To that I say, "So what?" Treat them with respect anyway. If they don't eventually reciprocate, you may need to cut that person out of your life. Yes, it's ok to cut toxic people out of your life, and it's necessary if we intend to live a positive and uplifting life ourselves.

We've also heard the old saying, "What goes around comes around," and that's another great way to think of the Golden Rule. What you give you get! Give good, get good. Give bad, get bad in return. What do you want to get? What would you like to receive? Do you want people to like you? Love you? Say good things about you? Want to be around you? If your answer to those questions was the obvious YES, YES, YES, YES, YES, YES, then you're human, and you should abide by the Golden Rule!

I completely understand that some people act in a manner where we sometimes feel like they don't deserve us to treat them well. Still I'm here to tell you that my philosophy on people like that has always been to treat them good anyway and hope it will rub off. In many cases it will, and that person will become more like you! Look at it this way; you could be the reason someone changes their attitude and how they treat others because of how you treat them. THAT'S EXCITING! Now get out there and treat others good today. NO MATTER WHAT!

Today's Challenge: Treat everyone with dignity and respect. Be friendly even if that person doesn't seem to deserve it. Watch as people start changing right before your eyes.

Positive Affirmation of the Day: I'm a great person, and I treat everyone with dignity and respect no matter what! (Do this in the mirror.)

Quote of the Day: "Do unto others as you would have them do unto you." —Matthew 7:12

Day Seven

Comfort Zone

LET'S GO RIGHT to the edge of our comfort zones today. Take the limits off your thoughts for today and think like a child again if only for a day. I promise you'll be happier by the end of the day. Eat some comfort food today, do something fun, and reward yourself for the last six days of working toward a new and better you!

Do you remember the way you thought when you were a kid? You likely thought you could be, do, and have anything. Most kids want to be teachers, doctors, lawyers, or professional athletes. Why? Because those are high-paying or rewarding careers everyone dreams of; kids aren't afraid to think and dream big! Most children, unlike adults, still believe they can do whatever comes to their minds. Why do children dream and think big, yet we develop a "settle for" mentality once we become adults?

It's simple when we are children; we haven't been beaten and knocked down by the world yet. As we age we start listening to all the naysayers in our lives, many of whom we love and trust. We hear "no" or "you can't do that" too often, and unfortunately we start to believe it. But today and beyond, let's get back to thinking like a child again and cozy up to the edge of our comfort zones. Thinking big can be scary and uncomfortable. I'm asking you to do it for a day and see how it makes you feel.

It's necessary to think like a child again when learning to develop a positive mindset. We have to take days to "dream" about what our lives would look like if we had no limitations. Is it realistic to have everything we want in life? Probably not. However we sure can have more of the things we want in this life if we take some time to "think like a child again" and remove all the restrictions from our thoughts.

Today's Challenge: Think great big today! What are some things you want to do, be, or have but have a hard time believing are possible? Think about doing, being, or having those things. Allow yourself to daydream about them, talk about them, write about them in your journal, then at the end of the day, smile and keep believing! Remember all great things start with belief!

Positive Affirmation of the Day: I will think like a child again; I can and will live my dreams! I'm unique; my life matters! (Do this in the mirror.)

Quote of the Day: "You never change your life until you step out of your comfort zone; change begins at the end of your comfort zone." —Roy T Bennett

DAY EIGHT

Always Be Learning

ZIG ZIGLAR TELLS a story of a graduation ceremony where he was speaking. He said he overheard one student say to another, "I'll never pick up another book until the day I die." Zig said those were the saddest words he'd ever heard. I agree with Zig.

The information I'm sharing in this book had to have come from somewhere, right? Yes, that's 100% correct! I've had to study motivation, positivity, and self-help for many years to get the kind of knowledge that it takes to write a book of this magnitude. The good news is that it starts with listening to one audio or reading one page of one good book. Any of us can do that, correct?

Hopefully you'll be like me and get hooked on living your best life and being joyful daily. How do you achieve an attitude of gratitude? How do you train your mind to wake up happy each day? How do you teach yourself to stay calm during the storms of life? For me the answer to those questions is simple.

You've got to wake up each day with a willingness to learn new things, buy the good book someone tells you about and read it, listen to the audio you heard about on social media, and click the link and watch the ten-minute video a friend sends you to brighten your day. It does start with little things just like those. Once you start doing those things daily, you'll form good learning habits, read, and listen to audios/videos daily. When you get to that point, you will have learned so many positive daily habits that it will be nearly impossible to be negative.

If anyone were to ask me what the secret to my success was, I'd say "to always be learning."

Here are a few ways you can learn more:

- Watch a video on something that interests you, anything.
- Listen to a podcast on a topic you want to know more about.
- Read; this can be a magazine, book, blog, or anything that interests you.
- Like and friend positive influencers on social media and read their content.
- Open and listen to or read any positive material friends/family/co-workers send you.

Today's Challenge: Do at least one of the things on the above list. Make it a goal today to learn something new you didn't know yesterday.

Affirmation of the Day: I want to learn new things today. I'm willing to go out of my way to do it. (Do this in the mirror.)

Quote of the Day: "Nothing we learn in this world is ever wasted." —Eleanor Roosevelt

Helping Others

TODAY'S MESSAGE IS all about helping others. One of the fastest ways to achieve our goals is to help others achieve theirs. Whenever we are helping others, we are also inevitably helping ourselves. ***REACH OUT AND HELP SOMEONE!***

The good news is there are so many ways to help others; something as simple as a smile can go a long way. Maybe it's helping a neighbor shovel the driveway or an older person at the grocery store with groceries. It could be as simple as talking to a friend going through a tough time and encouraging them. Volunteering at a hospital, nursing home, or your local city mission are all great ways to help others. If you look there are many ways we can reach out and help other people every day.

Please read today's quote of the day repeatedly throughout the day and try to break down and comprehend what Zig Ziglar is saying in that quote. He is telling us that by helping others, we also help ourselves. We want to help others for the right reason, but the fringe benefit is that it always comes back to us in the form of some blessing.

Today's Challenge: Go out of your way to do nice things for others, and smile at everyone you come in contact with today!

Positive Affirmation of the Day: I love helping others; it makes me feel so good! I will go out of my way to help others today! (Do this in the mirror.)

Quote of the Day: "You can have everything in life that you want, if you'll just help enough other people get what they want." —Zig Ziglar

Attitude of Gratitude

THERE ARE SO many things in our lives to be thankful for, and it's meaningful to take a little time each day to do just that. BE GRATEFUL! Have an attitude of gratitude. If we want to have more to give thanks for, we must first be grateful for what we already have.

The Bible tells us, "Give thanks in all circumstances: for this is God's will for you in Christ Jesus." —1 Thessalonians 5:18

I mean it's in the Bible, and whether you're a Christian or not, we'd all agree that the Bible is full of wisdom.

Developing positive habits like an attitude of gratitude is easier said than done. Our world is so full of negativity that sometimes it feels overwhelming. Because of that learning and using the positive habits taught in this book is so important. Once you start implementing some of these habits, you'll realize that you do have a lot to give thanks for. Being grateful also creates joy and happiness, and who doesn't want that?

During a time in my life when I was struggling with both anxiety and depression, Tara taught me to do a "gratitude journal." This is where you get a notebook. At the top of each page, you write "I'm thankful for" and then write down ten things that you are thankful for that day. It's incredible how quickly doing that changed my thinking and helped me realize how good my life was. I take it a step further and pray and thank God for the things I write down each day right afterward too. It is very gratifying to be grateful. Try it!

Dedication: Today's message was to thank my wife, Tara Wolbers. Keep encouraging people, Tara. I'm thankful to you! I love you!

Today's Challenge: Start a gratitude journal today. Write down ten things you're thankful for. If you like it as much as I did, keep doing it every day!

Positive Affirmation of the Day: I'm so happy and thankful that I woke up today. (Do this in the mirror.)

Quote of the Day: "Enjoy the little things, for one day you may look back and realize they were the big things." —Robert Brault

Day Eleven

Wake up on the "Right Side" of the Bed

WE'VE ALL HEARD and used the old expression, "Did you wake up on the wrong side of the bed today?" Why do we say that? That's right; we say it because someone is in a lousy mood, irritable, or just having a bad day. So if we can wake up on the wrong side of the bed some days, we can as easily decide to *"Wake up on the right side of the bed."* Am I right?

I have some good news. There are things we can and should be doing every morning when we first wake up that will help get our day off to a positive start. How the day starts is usually how the day will continue going. Have you found that too? Let's look at a few things we should and shouldn't be doing within the first half hour to an hour of waking up.

Things to Do: Look at some new, positive content. I know the first thing you're reaching for when you get up, if you're anything like me, is your phone. It's necessary to control the content you look at after waking up. Look at pages, websites, blogs, and podcasts that motivate and encourage you. Another excellent thing to do in the first hour of your day is to do a daily devotional or read a positivity journal like this one. Follow that up with positive affirmations, and you'll be ready to tackle whatever comes your way today! A quick walk or workout would also be wonderful before getting into the hustle and bustle of a new day!

Things to Avoid: Anything that can put you in a bad mood or ruin your day. Only you can decide what those things are. For many people checking your email or voicemails will get you thinking about what you have to get done today, and believe me there will be plenty of time later in each day to take care of those essential tasks! Dedicate the first half hour to an hour of your day to getting physically and mentally ready for a successful day.

Today's Challenge: Start developing new morning habits and do things that get your mind and body ready for the day ahead. Just try one or two of the things suggested above.

Positive Affirmation of the Day: My mornings are for positivity! I love waking up each day! (Do this in the mirror.)

Quote of the Day: "Lose an hour in the morning, and you will spend all day looking for it." —Richard Whately

Day Twelve

Have a Little Faith

I want to talk to you today about staying in faith during the ups and downs of life. Faith means "complete confidence in someone or something." Another definition says, "Strong belief in God or the doctrines of a religion, based on spiritual apprehension rather than proof." Belief, confidence, and trust are other words used to describe faith. I'm not sure about you, but I could use as many of those things as possible in my life!

Let's look at the first definition, which involves having faith in ourselves and others. This one can be very tricky. As humans we will make mistakes and let ourselves and others down at times. Does this mean we shouldn't believe in ourselves and those around us? NO WAY! Without this kind of faith, our lives would be miserable. I would caution you to understand that none of us is perfect. When someone lets us down or we let someone down, we should forgive and ask for forgiveness fast and then move on whenever possible, as unforgiveness is a recipe for an unhappy life.

Now let's examine the second definition. This one is my favorite. This type of faith involves believing in things before we can see them. I love this concept. The Bible (2 Corinthians 5:7) says, "Walk by faith, not by sight." What a fantastic idea, to believe in things yet unseen. This kind of faith is a spiritual faith, the type of faith Tara and I live by every day. This faith also brings us hope for the future, and it brings true joy and peace too. I sincerely hope you too have this kind of faith!

Today's Challenge: Tell someone you know and love that you believe in them today, and tell them you love them while you're at it. Doing so will help someone else to have faith in their fellow man and make you and them feel great!

Positive Affirmation of the Day: I will use my energy to trust, believe, and have faith today! (Do this in the mirror.)

Quote of the Day: "Faith is taking the first step, even when you don't see the whole staircase." —Martin Luther King Jr.

Faith definitions found in Oxford Languages Dictionary

Day Thirteen

Smile

WE ALL HAVE that person in our lives who always seems to be smiling and is just happy, happy, happy to be alive. So annoying, right? Just kidding. I love people who smile a lot, and I'm sure you do too! Who is that person in your life who is always wearing a smile? It probably made you smile just thinking of them. For me that person is my wife, Tara! She is the happiest person I know. (Maybe it's because she has me, ha!) Don't you love being around people like that? Doesn't it make you happier and put you in a better mood?

A smile is one of the best gifts we can give each other. Smiles are contagious, and they are free to give and receive! Try this sometime: intentionally smile at everyone you see for an hour or two and see how many smiles you get in return. I'll bet it will be almost 100%! Most people can't help but smile back; it's like a boomerang! Notice how good this makes you feel. The neat thing is that you will make other people feel that same way too! What is the feeling you'll be getting? HAPPINESS, and I can't think of a better emotion than that.

It's tough to be down or to have a bad day when you are constantly smiling at people. Most of them will smile right back at you, which is one of the best feelings we can get: to be appreciated enough by another person to get a big smile from them. It's so good for the soul! So will you start being the person everyone else loves being around? Do you want to be the person who helps lift people's spirits? Then start smiling more every day and watch as your relationships, mood, and overall outlook on life improve! SMILE, it is so good for you!

Today's Challenge: As recommended in today's reading, take an hour or two today and literally and intentionally smile at everyone you see. Count how many smiles you get in return, and at the end of the experiment, notice how much better it made you feel. The fringe benefit is that you'll be making others feel good too!

Positive Affirmation of the Day: I will smile more today because I'm happy! (Do this in the mirror.)

Quote of the Day: "Keep smiling, because life is a beautiful thing and there's so much to smile about." —Marilyn Monroe

DAY FOURTEEN

When the Going Gets Tough

WE'VE ALL HEARD the saying, "When the going gets tough, the tough get going." I've found that saying to be 100% true in my life. Have you? Tough people are that way for a reason! I'm not talking about physical toughness today. I'm referring to mental strength. But let's talk about physical strength first because it does relate. What do people have to do to become physically strong? They have to work out, right? Lift weights, do cardio, and spend hours each week doing things most people won't! So how do you think mental toughness develops? If you said the same way, you'd be correct. To get stronger mentally, we must constantly train our minds and spend hours each week doing things to improve our mental health and wellness, just like we'd have to do to become physically stronger.

I commend you for making it to day fourteen in this book. I guarantee that each day you continue to read and apply what's in these pages, you naturally gain mental toughness! You see doing things like this will build us mentally, and we have to be willing to do what most people aren't to get to the highest level of mental strength.

What are some things we can do to gain mental toughness? First we should read something positive daily (for example a book like this). Next we can listen to uplifting music and podcasts regularly. Spend some time in prayer and/or meditation, depending on your beliefs. And believe it or not, physical strength correlates to mental toughness, so we should exercise regularly; exercise is good for the mind.

If you are willing to do some things that most people won't, then I have excellent news for you. You will be in a select group of people who value their mental toughness. I'm living proof that when you are mentally tough, you'll have a leg up on the competition in anything you strive to do in life! Stay strong!

Today's Challenge: Read this page one more time today. Make sure it's in a quiet room where you can focus on what it says, then go out into the world mentally stronger and start to live your dreams. YOU CAN, AND YOU WILL!

Positive Affirmation of the Day: I'm willing to do what most people aren't to become mentally stronger. I'm a champion. (Do this in the mirror.)

Quote of the Day: "Champions aren't made in the gyms. Champions are made from something they have deep inside them—a desire, a dream, a vision." —Muhammad Ali

Day Fifteen

Repetition Is the Mother of Learning

Do you remember when you first learned how to ride a bike? Did you take off the first time you tried? Nope, you had to keep falling, then get back up and on the bike again for another try. Finally with tears in your eyes and bruises and bumps all over your little body, you did it. From then on you just jumped on your bike without fear, right?

You see life itself is a lot like learning to ride a bike; if we are willing to take the bumps and bruises, the pain, the agony of defeat, and, yes, even tears sometimes that the repetition of learning will bring us, then we can and will end up learning how to ride the bike of life.

Learning is simple: find something that works, keep practicing it, and learn how to perfect it. *REPETITION!* How much time do athletes dedicate to practice versus playing in real games? *REPETITION!* How much time do professional salespeople put into learning about their products and how to market them? *REPETITION!* How much time does a lawyer spend learning about the case before presenting it before a judge and jury? *REPETITION!* The answer to those questions is that, in most cases, they spend much more time preparing and learning how to play or perform than they spend doing that job!

We must learn this principle if we want to succeed at just about anything. *"Repetition is the mother of learning."* The more we practice something, the better we will do it!

One caution I'll give you, be sure you're studying and practicing the correct way of doing whatever it is you're learning. *"Practice doesn't make perfect. Perfect practice does!"* Find some good teachers and mentors and then get out there and get to learning and practicing today!

Today's Challenge: Start today. What is it you want to learn and get better at? Do it, and then do it again tomorrow, the next day, and on and on until you know it! *GET ON THAT BIKE!*

Positive Affirmation of the Day: I never give up; I will keep going until I get it right today! (Do this in the mirror.)

Quote of the Day: "Repetition is the mother of learning, the father of action, which makes it the architect of accomplishment." —Zig Ziglar

Positive by Association

I'VE HEARD THAT we become a lot like the five people we hang around the most. So before we get too far today, let's take a second to ask ourselves: Who are those five people in my life? Who am I becoming? Did the answers to those questions excite you or scare you?

There is an up and downside to today's conversation as, unfortunately, the title of today's message could also be "Negative by Association," correct? So which one is it for you in your life? Are the people you are around the most positive and uplifting people who speak life into you? Or is it the other way around? Are they a negative influence on your life?

Have you ever heard the quote, "If you can't change the people...change the people?" If we want to live our best life, full of joy in this crazy world, we must associate with positive people. I'm not suggesting that we be unrealistic about this either. I fully understand that we will all go through trials in life, and in no way am I telling anyone to abandon a friend or family member just because they are temporarily negative due to a circumstance in their life. Times like these are when we can use our positive attitude and influence to help them get through it.

However suppose you have people in your life who are habitually Debbie Downers, and they are bringing you down. I am 100% suggesting that you cut them out of your life or at least see far less of them, as it will eventually start to rub off on you. It's inevitable. If you're around negativity all the time, you become negative. If you're around positivity constantly, you become positive. PLAIN AND SIMPLE!

Today's Challenge: Take fifteen minutes to think about the people you are around the most in life. Rate them all from one–ten, with one being the most negative and ten being super positive. If the answers scare you, remember you CAN change the people.

Positive Affirmation of the Day: I positively influence the people around me! I attract positive people into my life! (Do this in the mirror.)

Quote of the Day: "Never underestimate the influence you have on others." —Laurie Buchanan

Train Like a Champion

WHAT IS THE difference between the average and high achievers in life? *Championship habits!* The best way to explain today's topic is to use sports as my reference, so here goes.

Why are some athletes so much better at their craft than others? Do they show up to practice a little earlier and stay a little later than their teammates? Are they going the extra mile compared to the average players, doing what others don't want to or won't do? Or are they just born better and more naturally gifted?

All exceptional athletes are naturally gifted; however that's not the most significant reason they stand out. Once athletes get to a certain level in any sport, everyone has natural ability. So let us examine why some players are so much better than the rest.

It's pretty simple. They develop championship habits and then do them when no one is watching! That's right. Most of what they do to become better than the rest, they do when no one else is around. They get there early and stay late, watch and scout their next opponent while everyone else has gone home, double down, and, as a result, they outperform everyone else and become known as the champions of the respective sport!

We, too, can develop these championship habits in our lives. But first we must be willing to show up early, stay late, and go the extra mile when no one else is watching! Have you heard the saying, "It's lonely at the top?" It's lonely because everyone else will have already left for the day, and the high achievers are left working alone.

Do you want to improve your job, move up the corporate ladder, excel at a hobby, or be a better spouse, parent, or friend? The answer is pretty simple.

Develop championship habits, and then do them when no one is watching! Do them every chance you get!

Today's Challenge: Look up some quotes about championship habits. You'll find out that today's message is 100% true, then take some time to decide which areas of your life you want to improve and get to work!

Positive Affirmation of the Day: I will train like a champion today; I'll show up early and stay late! (Do this in the mirror.)

Quote of the Day: "Champions don't become champions when they win an event, but in the hours, weeks, months, and years they spend preparing for it." —Michael Jordan

Burning Desire

TODAY LET'S TALK about desire. One definition says it is "a strong feeling of wanting to have something or wishing for something to happen." Another says desire is "a strong wish or want." Both definitions include wanting and/or wishing for something.

What is it you want or wish for? Do you crave it so bad that it keeps you up late at night and gets you up early in the morning thinking about it? Is what you want or wish for on your mind on and off all day? If so this is what I call a *"BURNING DESIRE."* Burning desire to me is wanting or wishing for something so badly that you are willing to do just about anything to get it!

We all have goals and dreams in our lives that fire us up! What fires you up? What gives you a burning desire? What is it that if you had or achieved, you'd be on top of the world? It all starts with knowing what it is you're super passionate about! Now that you're thinking about what excites you, I have a few more questions.

What are you doing about it? Do you have it written down? Have you taken some time and made a plan on how you're going to achieve it? Remember that you should be willing to do almost anything to achieve this. Finally have you taken any action toward getting or achieving what you desire?

A burning desire is the beginning of anything and everything exciting that has or will ever happen in our lives. For anything significant to happen, we must first be excited enough to take the necessary actions to achieve it! Desire alone may cut it with some goals, but believe me to achieve greatness, you'll need to take that passion to the next level and turn it into a burning desire!

Dedication: Today's message was inspired by a good friend and mentor of mine, Garry Robinson, who passed away on 1-17-22. Garry had a burning desire to help people; he helped me more than he ever knew.

Today's Challenge: Go back over today's message and take some time to think about what fires you up. Remember the first step is determining what we are most passionate about.

Positive Affirmation of the Day: I'm excited about _____! I'm going to do whatever it takes to achieve it. I have a burning desire! (Do this in the mirror.)

Quote of the Day: "The starting point in all achievement is desire." —Garry Robinson

Day Nineteen

If Today Was Your
Last Day

What if today was your last day? How would you live it? What would you do? Interesting questions to think about! Of course we'd all live differently today if we knew it would be our last day. We'd spend time with the people we love the most, eat our favorite foods, do our favorite things, and make sure everyone we love knew it! In other words we'd do what's most important!

It's so easy to get caught up in the hustle of life and forget what's most important to us. When we take some time to stop and think about what we'd do if we knew today would be our last day, we better understand where our real priorities lie and possibly live each day at least a little differently.

I'm not suggesting that we believe today will be our last, but rather that we live each day like we are dying. Country music superstar Tim McGraw's song "Live Like You Were Dying" says it best. In the chorus it says, "I went skydiving, I went Rocky Mountain climbing, I went 2.7 seconds on a bull named Fu Manchu, and I loved deeper, and I spoke sweeter, and I gave forgiveness I'd been denying, someday I hope you get the chance to live like you were dying."

We all have responsibilities every day, and in no way, shape, or form am I saying that we should ignore the ordinary tasks necessary in our daily lives. I recommend you live each day to the fullest, smile more, listen to music that moves you, tell people you love them, have fun, and eat the darn dessert (you know you want it). Hopefully today isn't our last day; however we never know when that day will come, so live today with enthusiasm, have some fun, get some things accomplished, and remember to give thanks for today because every day is a gift.

Today's Challenge: Tell someone you love them today, do something fun, and eat some dessert; you deserve it.

Positive Affirmation of the Day: I will live today to the fullest. I'm so thankful for each day. (Do this in the mirror.)

Quote of the Day: "Someday I hope you get the chance to live like you were dying." —Tim McGraw

Day Twenty

Keep on Keeping On

It's DAY TWENTY of this ninety-day quest for a better life; I'd like to congratulate you on still being here and for making it this far. However the journey is just beginning! One of my mentors from when I started my sales career almost thirty years ago always said, *"Keep on keeping on."*

I was very young (eighteen years old) and new to sales. I was also very motivated and often wondered why we kept hearing, *"Keep on keeping on."* After my second full year in the business, I began understanding what it meant and why it was said so often. My mentor knew what I had yet to learn, that life was hard and challenges would arise; he also knew what a sales slump felt like and that people would quit when the going got tough. I was young and excited, and life hadn't knocked me down yet. Yes, I said yet!

So if challenges arise, you're in a slump or life is just plain hard right now. DON'T GIVE UP; NEVER GIVE UP! Keep reading this book every day for the entire ninety days. *KEEP ON KEEPING ON!* If there is one thing I know for sure, life will bring challenges, and mental and physical preparedness is imperative! How do we do that? Well, you're already off to a good start; keep reading these messages, doing the challenges and positive affirmations, and reading the quotes that go with each day. Keep preparing your body, mind, and spirit to conquer the obstacles life will put in your path. Keep developing the mindset of a winner. One thing we know about champions is that they all had to go through tough times but never gave up! *Keep on keeping on!*

Today's Challenge: Take a minute to reflect on these first twenty days and pat yourself on the back. Think about how the way you think is already changing, and then *KEEP ON KEEPING ON!*

Positive Affirmation of the Day: I get going when the going gets tough! I'm physically and mentally strong, and I'm getting stronger every day! (Do this in the mirror.)

Quote of the Day: "It does not matter how slowly you go as long as you do not stop." —Confucius

Day Twenty-One

Do It Now

I've learned over the years that the best time to do the most important tasks of the day, week, month, or year is *NOW!!!* It's so much easier to procrastinate and say I'll do it tomorrow, next week, or next month, but we all know what that means, right? It's not going to get done!

My dad, who has also been an excellent business mentor, taught me many years ago how to avoid putting important things off. Are you ready for this? It's a simple thing to do, but it's vital if you want to become successful and stay on task toward attaining your goals and dreams. Here it is: ***make a to-do list every day of the things you need to get done that day***, then prioritize that list and do the most important things first. At the end of the day, if you complete the entire list, that's fantastic. However there will be days when you don't. What do you do then? Well, do what my dad taught me: make a new list for tomorrow, and that list will start with the things you couldn't get done today.

Today's message was simple, but having a daily to-do list will keep you organized and on task. Being organized and staying on task is imperative to becoming or remaining successful.

A little more about my dad, he and my mom are responsible for getting me into sales all those years ago. We are still in that same business today. How have we stayed in the same industry for so long and been so successful, you ask? We've always been very organized, known what's essential for us daily, and had a *"DO IT NOW"* mentality! One more tidbit about my parents: they are very successful due to being highly disciplined and always willing to learn new things and change even when change is unpopular or uncomfortable!

Dedication: Today's writing honors my parents, Justin and Sharon Wolbers. Thank you for mentoring me and being great business leaders and parents. I love you both dearly.

Today's Challenge: Make a to-do list and do the most important things first. Whatever you don't get done today, put it on tomorrow's list as the priority.

Positive Affirmation of the Day: I have a do-it-now mentality! (Do this in the mirror.)

Quote of the Day: "Do it now, sometimes later becomes never." —Anonymous

DAY TWENTY-TWO

Win the Day!

TODAY I WANT to challenge you to focus on living one day at a time. The Bible says in Psalm 118: 24, "This is the Day that the Lord has made; let us rejoice and be glad in it." Today is a gift; open it, and use it to the fullest!

Rejoice and be glad you're alive! I completely understand you may be going through some trials in your life, but focus today on something positive that comes out of the day. Even if it's just one thing, pick it, run with it, and give thanks for it! *WIN THE DAY!*

Our nephew passed away in April 2015 at fifteen years old after a year-long battle with cancer. His name was Austin "Flash" Schroeder. Austin dealt with pain daily during his struggle and was still absolutely 100% determined to *WIN THE DAY* every day. His family adopted this mantra during his battle and lived it every day. They always looked for the good (the bad was pretty obvious), so their philosophy was to focus on the positive! If a fourteen–fifteen-year-old fighting cancer and his family can find the good every day, what's our excuse? The answer is that we don't have a reason good enough!

Austin's family has continued to carry the *WIN THE DAY* attitude every day since he went to be with the Lord. They are some of the most positive and uplifting people, and we love being around them as they are ALWAYS looking for the good in every situation!

Today and every day, look for the good (the bad is always apparent), so be the kind of person constantly searching for the positive things that happen and then be sure to give thanks for anything good that happens each day. (This is where a gratitude journal comes in handy.)

Dedication: To Austin "Flash" Schroeder. We love and miss you.

Today's Challenge: When your day is coming to a close and you're getting ready for bed, sit down for fifteen minutes and write down five things you're thankful for that happened today. You'll be surprised at how much you come up with! You may even write more than five. If you start doing this daily, that's a "gratitude journal."

Positive Affirmation of the Day: I'm happy and grateful for another day to be alive. I will look for the positive today! I will WIN THE DAY! (Do this in the mirror.)

Quote of the day: "Don't let what you cannot do interfere with what you can do." —John R Wooden

DAY TWENTY-THREE

Feel the Fear, and Do It Anyway

YEARS AGO I had a pretty severe bout with anxiety and depression. Late one night I was lying in bed worried sick (that was every night for me back then). I saw an infomercial promoting a program to help with anxiety and depression. I thought, "I can't afford the $500, but I'm sick and tired of being sick and tired." So I put the $500 on my credit card, and the program was in my hands a week later.

I'm not writing today to promote that particular program. However I learned a principle through the program I've been using and teaching ever since. The concept is simple. *"Feel the fear, and do it anyway."* How many things have you put off or just not done in your life because of fear? If you're anything like me, fear of loss, failure, and rejection has probably held you back from doing many things you wanted or needed to do. Well, that stops today!

Want to change careers, but you're afraid to? Feel the fear, and do it anyway! Want to ask someone on a date, but you're fearful of rejection? Feel the fear, and do it anyway! Want to start your own company, but you're afraid to fail? Feel the fear, and do it anyway! Want to _____, but you're scared of _____? Fill in the blanks with what you want and why you fear it, then *FEEL THE FEAR, AND DO IT ANYWAY!*

Always remember that we only get one chance to live the life God gave us. Why live in fear of what could go wrong? Instead of asking yourself what could go wrong, start asking these questions. What could go right? What if I do it? What if I'm successful? What if they say YES? What if it works even better than I

45

thought it would? I'm not suggesting going out and doing something crazy without taking the proper time to think and research it, but I am suggesting living your life with hopeful optimism rather than fear! You'll still have fear no matter what, but from now on, you'll feel that fear and then do it anyway!

Today's Challenge: Think about one thing you've been putting off because of fear. Then instead of asking yourself, what if I fail? Ask yourself, what if I succeed?

Positive Affirmation of the Day: I will allow myself to feel the fear today, but I'm not letting that stop me from doing what I want. (Do this in the mirror.)

Quote of the Day: "Feel the fear, and do it anyway." —Susan Jeffers

Day Twenty-Four

Laugh a Little

WHAT IF I told you there is something out there that can improve our immune systems, relieve pains, increase satisfaction, and improve moods? What if I also told you that it was free and available to all of us? Would you want to know what it is? Of course you would!

*LAUGHTER **is what I'm referring to!*** The things listed above are just the long-term positive effects on our health, according to the Mayo Clinic.

(Source: mayoclinic.org Stress relief from laughter? It's no joke —Mayo Clinic)

Mayo also states in the same article that laughing is a great form of stress relief; it activates and relieves our stress response and soothes tension! Laughing enhances our intake of oxygen-rich air, which stimulates our hearts, lungs, and muscles. If that isn't enough reason to laugh more, it's also increasing the endorphins released by our brains—and endorphins trigger a positive feeling in the body. They are known as a "happy hormone." I don't know about you, but these are all things I want as much of as I can get!

So starting today be more intentional about doing things that make you laugh. It could help you live longer, and it WILL help you live happier! If you are smiling and laughing more often, what does that do for the most important people in your life? If you said it makes them feel better and want to be around you more, then you read my mind! Laughing helps relationships too!

Today's Challenge: This one is going to be fun. Watch a sitcom, funny YouTube video, or comedian today, and don't hold back! LAUGH IT UP!

Positive Affirmation of the Day: I will intentionally laugh more today; it's good for me. (Do this in the mirror.)

Quote of the Day: "Laughing is, and always will be, the best form of therapy." —Dau Voire

Together Everyone Achieves More

ONE OF MY favorite acronyms for TEAM is the title for today's message, and I truly believe that ***Together Everyone Achieves More!*** Today I want to talk about teamwork. Are you currently part of any team? Sports? Work? Home? There are all different types of teams in life. It starts when we are children and then carries on throughout our lives. Here are a couple of questions I want you to ask yourself today.

Am I a team player? Would I want myself as a teammate? Am I currently on a team that is making a difference? The better we work with a group, the higher our chances of success. We'd have to be Superman or Wonder Woman to get through the trials of life alone. Think about all the successful athletes in the world; they all have one thing in common. They were phenomenal individually; however they would've been nothing without the supporting cast around them. Even in an individual sport like golf, the professionals have a team. They have coaches and trainers who help them get better every day.

Are you married or in a relationship? Do you have a family? Do you work somewhere where it's more than just you there? Do you use an accountant for your business? Do you have an investment firm helping you with your money? If you answered yes to any of those questions, you are on a team and should be pouring into the people around you, trying to help them. Your life will be much easier when they are happy and feel appreciated!

Whether leading a team or following a coach or business leader, I've always believed that my contribution should make an impact. Do everything in your power to help with the success of any team you may currently be a part of. Too many players on teams coast through the practices of life, and those are the players that won't be on the team for long. Do your best to make an impact every day; your coach, leader, or followers will thank you.

Today's Challenge: Go out of your way at home, work, and anywhere else you feel like you're part of a team to help as many people as you can today! Be a TEAM PLAYER today.

Positive Affirmation of the Day: I'm a TEAM PLAYER! I love being a great teammate! (Do this in the mirror.)

Quote of the Day: "I want to be an impact player on a team that makes a difference." —Chris Roberts

DAY TWENTY-SIX

Giving Is Living

HAVE YOU EVER donated your time or money to your favorite charity, cause, or a person or family in need? How did that make you feel? I'm going to guess that you probably felt pretty awesome about it. There is just something special about giving, isn't there? It just feels so good and so right; *GIVING IS LIVING.* The beautiful thing about giving is that we can do it in so many ways.

If you are fortunate enough to have been blessed financially, you may be the person who likes to donate money to your favorite charities, causes, or people in need. Or you could be the kind of person who is more "hands on," and in that case, you're more apt to donate your time and energy to a cause. Whether money or your time, it's a beautiful thing to do, and all charitable organizations need both money and volunteers to be able to do whatever their mission is.

Here is the best news! When we give, it always seems to find its way back to us tenfold. The Bible says in Luke 6:38, "Give, and it will be given to you. A good measure, pressed down, shaken together, and running over, will be poured into your lap. For with the measure you use, it will be measured to you." I don't know how you interpret that scripture, but I believe it says that when we give, we will later receive! That's quite the promise. Tara and I have found this scripture to be 100% true in our lives. We also believe that you can't out-give God.

Lastly there are other very subtle and simple ways we can give of ourselves. We can offer a smile or a compliment. We can pay for the car behind us in the drive-thru, donate our time at a local mission or nursing home, or even help build a home with Habitat for Humanity. We can be a blessing in many ways in our local communities and the world. Find your favorite way to bless a person or an organization today. *Giving is living!*

Today's Challenge: Go out of your way today to bless someone. Remember even a smile or a compliment is a way of giving.

Positive Affirmation of the Day: I'm a giving person and will do what I can today to help others. (Do this in the mirror.)

Quote of the Day: "Only by giving are you able to receive more than you already have." —Jim Rohn

Change Equals Progress

CAN YOU IMAGINE what our world would look like today if people weren't open to change? We'd still be living in caves and hunting for food. ***Change is necessary*** but can also be intimidating and downright scary.

We used to go to "The Video Store" to rent movies. Now we stream our movies from our smart TV. Before the invention of the cell phone, we used the landline phone from our homes when we wanted to make plans with friends or family. Now we pick up our cell phones and text each other from anywhere. That was less than thirty years ago; think about the changes we've made in just those two examples! It's called progress; without change it would come to a screeching halt.

So the next time you feel uncomfortable due to life changes, remember that ***change equals progress.*** Also remember that most changes will come with challenges and bring at least some discomfort. Change is uncomfortable until we get used to it. The good news is that we adjust and get used to it, moving on with the change as it becomes our new normal. So feel that fear of changing, but do it anyway. As I say in many of these messages, you'll thank yourself later.

Today's Challenge: Think back over the past year or two, and remember the changes you had to make that are now simply the new normal. Remember how it felt, and then remind yourself it was worth it.

Positive Affirmation of the Day: I'm open to positive changes in my life. Change brings me progress. (Do this in the mirror.)

Quote of the Day: "To improve is to change; to be perfect is to change often."
—Winston Churchill

Day Twenty-Eight

Goals...Do You Have Them?

WOULD YOU EVER go on a vacation without planning it first? Would you leave for a road trip without a good GPS? Those questions seem silly because no one would do either. But most people are going on life's journey without using GPS, formal planning, or a roadmap... What is this roadmap I'm referring to that would give us better direction in our lives? *GOALS...do you have them?*

Most of us spend days, weeks, and sometimes even months planning our next vacation. So how can we go through something as complex as life without proper planning, preparation, or a roadmap for success? Zig Ziglar used to say, "Don't become a wandering generality. Be a meaningful specific." I know that quote can seem confusing, so put it this way. Zig implied that a person with no goals wanders, hoping good things will happen. While people with goals have done some planning and therefore have a roadmap for success and can expect good things to happen.

If you're into sports, this analogy may hit home for you. How much fun would a basketball game be without a backboard or hoop? How fun would football be with no field goals or touchdowns? How about soccer? How much fun would it be with no ball? These scenarios would involve people running aimlessly in cool uniforms with no objective. Let's take the scoreboard away and play without keeping the score. How boring would that be? Fans would stop showing up overnight. Why? It's simple: no one would show up because we just took the objective out of the game; there would be no real reason to play, would there? Neither team could win!

Life is a lot like the sports mentioned above; it's more fun and fulfilling if we have an objective we aim for, a SCOREBOARD... Otherwise known as GOALS... So I ask you again, do you have them? If so that's great; keep it up. If not turn the page, and I'll help you tomorrow. Today I covered why goals are essential. Tomorrow I'll give you a simple proven system for setting goals. See you then!

Today's Challenge: Write down five things you want to do, be, or have. Start brainstorming today. You'll need it for tomorrow.

Positive Affirmation of the Day: My life has a purpose, and I'm willing to do whatever it takes to find what it is and then chase it! (Do this in the mirror.)

Quote of the day: "Goals are like magnets. They'll attract the things that make them come true." —Tony Robbins

Five Steps to Your Future Goals

YESTERDAY'S CHALLENGE WAS to write down five things you want to do, be, or have. If you took that challenge and did that, **CONGRATULATIONS**... You just took the first step toward setting goals! Today I'm giving you some steps to help you develop new goals and start living the life you deserve. If you already have clearly defined goals, that's fantastic; this will be a good refresher. The following steps work best over five days, so return to day twenty-nine for the next step. Here we go.

The Five-Day Process

Day One: Think about things you want to do, be, or have. After some thought make a list as short or long as you want. *Stop now and make a list.*

Day Two: Categorize the list you made yesterday by how long it will take to achieve each goal and separate them into the three categories listed below. It's essential to do this step to ensure your goals are balanced and don't contradict one another.

1. *Short term—one month to one year*
2. *Midterm—one to five years*
3. *Long term—anything longer than five years*

Day Three: Review the list. Take time to relook at every goal you wrote down, and remove the ones that don't excite you. We do this step to ensure we still feel good about and want what's on the list a few days after writing them down. It's ok to remove some; simply cross them off the list.

Day Four: Write down your top three goals from each category. These will be the goals we will focus on moving forward. Take some time to write a short plan to achieve each of these nine goals. This will take a little time, but then again so does planning a vacation, and we all do that without even giving it a second thought, right? What we are doing now is much more critical; we are planning your life and future success! You'll be glad you took some time on this step when you're living your dreams later. If you start to get frustrated on this step, that's normal. Move on to the next goal, and revisit the one you're struggling with. It will be easier to develop a plan for some goals than others.

Day Five: Take action; start a goal journal where you write these nine goals down either in the morning when you first wake up or at night just before bed. (A goal journal is simply a spiral notebook.) You want these goals to be on your mind constantly, so look at them daily. Now it's time to start following the plans you made in step four. We made those plans for a reason. TO TAKE ACTION AND ACHIEVE OUR GOALS! *Do this on day five and every day after.*

Important: Once you achieve some of these goals. Please return to this exercise, do it again, and keep setting new goals to replace the ones you reach. Also you can do one of two things if you don't hit a goal. Either select a new date and keep working toward that goal, or forget that goal and set a new one to work for. It's also essential to set a deadline—a date by which you want to achieve it—and write it next to each goal. Deadlines make goals more specific and measurable, give you a timetable to work with, and help you know if you're on track for achieving each goal. Lastly if you ever feel like you're not motivated by your goals, it's ok to scratch that goal off your list and make a new one to replace it. I've always found it very important to have at least some short-, mid-, and long-term goals to work toward!

Bonus Thought: I've found in my many years of teaching goals that everyone will be motivated differently. With short-term goals, some people need daily goals, and others perform better using weekly or monthly goals. Some people even like using a one-year timeframe as a minimum. But I know for sure that *EVERYONE* performs better when they use a mix of short-, mid-, and long-term goals. Short-term goals act as stepping stones to reaching the midterm, while mid-term goals act as stepping stones to achieving long-term targets.

Today's Challenge: Take the next five days to do this goal program!

Positive Affirmation of the Day: I believe in myself and can do this goal program. I'm going to live my dreams. (Do this in the mirror.)

Quote of the Day: "The path to success is to take massive, determined actions."
—Tony Robbins

Think Outside the Box

HAVE YOU EVER had someone tell you to "stop overthinking"? Have you ever said that to anyone? If you have don't feel bad, we've all said it. Most of us are more prone to "underthinking." To tell someone to stop overthinking is to ask them to stop trying to figure something out; in most cases that's terrible advice.

The better way to help ourselves and others when we are dealing with situations and/or decisions in our lives that can lead to what we call "over-thinking" would be to say *"change your thinking"* or *"start thinking outside the box."* In truth the worst thing we can do in these times when our thoughts just aren't working is to stop thinking. If our current thought process isn't getting us the results we are looking for, it's not time to stop thinking; it's simply time to change the course of our thoughts and try something new and maybe even something outside of our comfort zone. *THINK OUTSIDE THE BOX!*

Overthinking is real; however we should change our thinking rather than stop thinking altogether. Our minds will always be racing with thoughts whether we like it or not. Let's control and intentionally change these thoughts when the current thought process reaches a dead end.

Same old thoughts = same old results!
New thought processes = changes and new results!

So what are you waiting for? Change your thoughts today and watch the new and improved results! Think outside the box!

Today's Challenge: Pick anything in your life that you've been struggling with and change the way you think about it. Ask a few trusted people for their opinion, which may help you think outside the box.

Positive Affirmation of the Day: I'm open to changing my thoughts to improve my life! (Do this in the mirror.)

Quote of the Day: "We can't solve problems by using the same kind of thinking we used when we created them." —Albert Einstein

Day Thirty-One

Gratitude Journal

HAVE YOU EVER had one of those days when it seemed like nothing went as you planned or expected? Have you ever had the opposite happen, where everything seemed to go exactly how you wanted or planned? Of course we've all had days we would prefer to forget and just as many days where we were so high on cloud nine, we thought we'd never come back down.

Which of those days do you focus on more? The good or the bad? The human instinct, for some reason, makes it easier to focus on those days we should forget about and to forget about the days we should be talking and reminiscing about. We must train our minds to look for the positive each day and release or forget about the negativity! Yes, you read that right, and one of the best ways I've found to do this is to use a *GRATITUDE JOURNAL* every day.

What exactly is a gratitude journal, you ask? It's a simple habit we can all learn that takes less than five minutes each day. All you have to do is learn it and then develop the habit of doing it daily! I'll explain.

Get a spiral notebook or any lined journal, and each day either in the morning when you first wake up or at night before going to bed, get it out! At the top of a new page every day, write: "Today I'm thankful for..." Then underneath that write as few or as many things as you want to. Below is an example of what it could look like if you wrote down five things. I chose to be generic for the example. Remember it's your gratitude journal, and you can write whatever you want to!

Today I'm Thankful For
My Spouse, My kids, My job, My pet, My car

Something about constantly writing down the things you're thankful for each day makes it easier to be happy. It's like magic for the mind. Even on a rough day, I guarantee you'll still find many things you're grateful for! (Oxygen, electricity, gas, clean drinking water, coffee, clean clothing, etc.)

Today's Challenge: Start a gratitude journal. Don't wait any longer to live a happier life!

Positive Affirmation of the Day: I'm thankful for everything God has given me. (Do this in the mirror.)

Quote of the Day: "Gratitude is riches, complaint is poverty." —Doris Day

Day Thirty-Two

Leaders Are Learners

HAVE YOU EVER heard the quote, "Not all readers are leaders, but all leaders are readers?" I'd amend that to say, "Not all leaders are readers, but the good ones must be!" A good leader knows their number one priority is to help their team reach their full potential and grow. The best leaders I know are constantly looking for better ways to do things so they can go out and teach their teams how to improve. The most significant difference between a leader and a follower mentality is that leaders learn intending to teach, while followers learn so they can do it themselves.

How can we get better without knowing more all the time? The answer is that we can't! How can we lead others without constantly learning more ourselves? Once again we can't! Do you want to be a leader? You have to be a learner first!

A good friend of mine always says, "Learn it, then do it, and only then can we teach it!" I love that idea because it has the priorities in the correct order. And guess what? After we teach it enough, we can master it.

I've heard that good leaders must first be good followers, so just because you may not be leading others right now doesn't mean you won't be someday. Be a good follower now; you never know where that will "lead" (pun intended).

Good leaders put a lot of time into learning to improve themselves, and then they pay it forward and help their teams! To lead you must first have leadership habits; one of those critical habits is always learning!!! *LEADERS ARE LEARNERS!*

Today's Challenge: Read a few pages in a book on a subject you're interested in. Do this every day, and you can start doing new things, and eventually you'll be the leader teaching others all that you've learned. *I double-dog dare you!*

Positive Affirmation of the Day: I'm willing to learn something new today; I'm a leader! (Do this in the mirror.)

Quote of the Day: "The best leaders were once the best followers." —Anonymous

Develop Healthy Habits

ACCORDING TO THE *Merriam-Webster* dictionary, a habit is "a usual way of behaving: something that a person does often in a regular and repeated way."

We all have habits; some are conscious habits that we do intentionally every day, and some are unconscious habits that we do automatically without even thinking. All routines are one of two things for us: good or bad. Today I want to focus on the conscious habits of life, the practices we intentionally do every day. If we change our mindful habits to be healthier and more positive, our unconscious habits will change over time too.

So what are you doing in a regular and repeated way? Are the habits you've formed having a positive or negative effect on your life? These are essential questions to ask ourselves. The patterns we are developing now will affect or infect us next week, month, year, or even the rest of our lives. Let's ensure they positively affect our lives rather than infect us negatively.

If the habits you've developed are healthy and positive, taking you where you want to be in life, STAY THE COURSE! However if you feel like the habits you've developed are unhealthy and not good for you, then start making small changes each day. Remember it's the small changes over time that lead to significant changes long term. If you focused on getting better at something daily, how good would you be one, five, or even ten years from now? The answer is obvious, right? YOU'D BE AN EXPERT! Habits work the same way as skills; if you want them to be healthy and positive, you must work at them every day. The good news is that you don't have to make significant changes; regular small ones will get you where you want to go!

What's the best way to live life? One day at a time! Yesterday is gone;

tomorrow may or may not even come; live for TODAY! Today matters, and small changes in your daily habits will transform your life!

Today's Challenge: Take some time to think about and write down some of your current habits. For example spiritual, family, friends, diet, exercise, work, social media, etc. After doing that think about ways to improve little by little in each area, then start!

Positive Affirmation of the Day: Change is good for me; I want to change my habits today! (Do this in the mirror.)

Quote of the Day: "Motivation is what gets you started, habit is what keeps you going." —Jim Rohn

Whatever It Takes

AT TWENTY-TWO HE went bankrupt after the failure of a cartoon series in Kansas City; he wanted to become an actor, but that also failed. A newspaper once fired him for having a lack of imagination and creativity. After multiple failures in life, he designed the famous character: MICKEY MOUSE! Walt Disney didn't give up and did whatever it took!

A struggling writer and divorcee, at thirty-one years old, she was a single mom on welfare and could barely afford to feed her child. She was financially ruined. Her manuscript got rejected multiple times. What manuscript was it? You may have heard of it. HARRY POTTER! J. K. Rowling wouldn't give up and did whatever it took! She is now worth over a billion dollars!

While many of us may never experience the wild success of Walt Disney or J. K. Rowling, we can succeed in our chosen venture! Just remember that everyone successful has had moments where they just didn't quit, and that's why they made it!!! Disney and Rowling did whatever it took.

Most successful people are very *disciplined,* have a great *work ethic,* have clearly defined *goals* with a *plan of action* to achieve them, and *have great daily habits.* Many do *positive affirmations,* have *great attitudes,* and are constantly *learning* new things to improve themselves. Successful people also have *faith and hope* and understand that great things don't happen overnight, and therefore *they don't quit* just because the going gets tough.

Successful people aren't usually afraid of *change; they* know it's necessary for progress, and champions *think outside the box* because they know that that's where true success is waiting. Most also have an *attitude of gratitude* and understand that *giving is living; they* realize they wouldn't be near as successful without all the support of those around them. They are *team players!*

While all of the qualities listed above are important to winning in life, and the successful people I know are doing them, the most important thing is being willing to do whatever it takes to succeed and having a never-give-up attitude. Walt Disney and J. K. Rowling went through tough times and certainly didn't give up…you shouldn't either…*DO WHATEVER IT TAKES!!!*

Today's Challenge: Go to your favorite search engine and research stories of people who never gave up, read about them! The stories will inspire you!

Positive Affirmation of the Day: I'll do whatever it takes today to achieve my goals. (Do this in the mirror.)

Quote of the Day: "Our greatest weakness lies in giving up. The most certain way to succeed is always to try just one more time." —Thomas Edison

Day Thirty-Five

Problem or Opportunity

Do you have any problems that you're currently dealing with? Of course you do; we all do! Unfortunately problems are just part of our daily lives. What if instead of panicking, freaking out, or ignoring them, we could find a way to look at problems differently? What if when a problem arises, we would decide whether we would resolve it or not, we would at least learn from it, or we would turn the problem into an opportunity to learn, improve, and help others? Would our lives be a little easier if we looked at a problem with that mindset? I think so! Problems can be opportunities to improve lives.

Problems will usually fit into one of two categories. First we have minor problems, then more significant issues. Before we get too far, we must look at each situation and decide whether it's minor or major. How we'll deal with minor vs. significant issues is quite different. A small problem is usually easy to deal with, and by the end of the day, it's forgotten, as it wasn't that big of a deal. This kind of problem differs from the one we'll look at today.

It's the significant problems in life I'd like to focus on. These are the more serious issues that arise in our lives. They range from sickness to the loss of a loved one, to a trust issue in a relationship, fear of job/income loss, legal challenges, tax issues, etc. None of us want these kinds of problems, but we all have to deal with them at some point in our lives. So if you're dealing with one now, you're not alone. With the significant issues in life, if we take a different approach, we change our mindset from worry, anxiety, depression, and spite. Then we dig deep and start looking for opportunities to learn, grow, and help others from them. We can not only change and improve our lives, but also our communities and world.

My brother and sister-in-law, Craig and Stacy Schroeder, found out in early 2014 that their oldest child, Austin, had cancer. Unfortunately on April 28th of 2015, Austin passed away. That could and would, for many people, be the end of the story, but not for the Schroeders. They decided to make a difference and, in the process, found a way to make Austin's light continue to shine in this world. They founded "The Fight With Flash Foundation" to help raise funds to research adolescent and young adult (AYA) cancer. Their charity has raised and donated over $582,000 and counting at the time of this writing (2022). It has helped researchers at the University of Iowa Stead Family Children's Hospital learn more about how to save children like Austin in the future. While we can't bring Austin back, the Schroeders decided to take a traumatic time they experienced in their lives and make a difference in other people's lives. Now that's what I call turning a problem into an opportunity to make a difference.

So the next time you're facing a more serious problem, take some time to think about how you can use it as an opportunity to learn, grow, and help others.

Today's Challenge: Pray for people facing significant problems today; they need it!

Positive Affirmation of the Day: My problems are opportunities. (Do this in the mirror.)

Quote of the Day: "In the middle of difficulty lies opportunity." —Albert Einstein

You Matter

I SEE YOU, and I know how you feel; I understand. Life is tough; you may be having a tough day today or going through a tough season. Is that you? Are you the one I'm talking to right now? Is life challenging right now? Things are not going your way, no matter what you do, no matter what you say. It just seems like life keeps going down the wrong path.

If this is you, I know how you feel; I've been in that spot where it didn't feel like anything could go my way. I'm here to tell you, if nobody else has, keep going and don't give up! The only way you lose in this life is if you quit, and you're not a quitter; you weren't born a quitter. KEEP ON GOING!

God made you on purpose and for a purpose, maybe you just haven't found yours or you've lost sight of it. I know that when I was at my lowest point in life, I lost my purpose. Positive changes started happening when I reconnected with God and the people closest to me who wanted me to improve.

If you're at a crossroads like this in your life, staying connected to people who will be uplifting and positively influence you is crucial. Read good, uplifting material daily, watch positive videos, set and go after some new and exciting goals, and be grateful for all the good things you still have in your life. Stay in faith, and keep your hopes high; your rebound is right around the corner as long as you believe it is. Your mind is a powerful tool; using it to your advantage during difficult times is imperative.

Whether your life is going wonderful or not, I want to remind you today that *YOU MATTER*, your life matters, you're important, people love you, and you're here for a reason. GOD BLESS YOU! God put you on this earth on purpose, for a purpose! If you're the one who needed to read this today, I'm glad you are here!

One more time read this part out loud, *YOU...*yes, I did say *YOU...YOU MATTER*, you're important, your life matters, and you're loved! Always remember that!!!

Today's Challenge: Pray, and thank God for your current situation, good or bad. Remember we learn the most during the trials of life, so be thankful either way.

Positive Affirmation of the Day: I matter, my life matters, I'm loved, God made on purpose, for a purpose. (Do this in the mirror.)

Quote of the Day: "You were seen, you were heard, and you matter." —Oprah Winfrey

Are You Having Fun?

DO YOU REMEMBER when you were a child and didn't have a care in the world? What was life all about in those younger years? What did you think about the most? If you were anything like me, you were probably most interested in having fun. Our biggest concern was waking up excited about our life every morning, getting out of bed, and looking for a toy, video game, sport, or a friend to play with. The reason we had an easier time focusing on having fun when we were young is simple. We didn't have the stress that comes with age; those challenges don't typically set in until the teenage or young adult years.

Life changes and teenage and young adult years can take a toll on us. School, grades, jobs, and life responsibilities start to set in. In many cases this is where we first experience stress, anxiety, and sometimes even depression. All three of those things make it harder to enjoy life. Then come the adult years and the responsibilities that come with careers, running a household, relationships, and families. Don't get me wrong, these are beautiful times of life, but for many they create even more stress, anxiety, and, in some cases, depression, making it harder to enjoy life and have fun.

So how do we balance the challenges of the teenage, young adult, and finally the adult years of life and still find ways to enjoy our lives? The answer to that question can be a little different for everyone because we all have different personalities, and I can only tell you what works for me! So here goes!

I wake up every morning and immediately pray, thanking God for everything and everyone He's given me in my life (see day ten). I do positive affirmations (see day two), I write in a gratitude journal daily (see day thirty-one), I look at my goals every day (see days twenty-eight and twenty-nine), and I focus on pouring into every meaningful relationship in my life (this isn't always easy; you have to make time for it). When it comes to ensuring my life stays interesting, I plan things I enjoy doing each week (I'm big into sports and music, so I put games and concerts into my schedule). So I schedule fun into my life. You won't have the same likes as me; use your imagination and plan some things you enjoy, but do it every week. Not a week should go by that you don't intentionally do something fun.

Life will have its ups and downs, no matter what we do or how we live. Today I'm suggesting that since we already know that life will have stressful days and seasons, why don't we plan to have fun through it all? Why don't we understand that life will throw us challenges but realize we can still enjoy it? What are you waiting for? Get after it, and plan something fun for tomorrow.

Today's Challenge: Plan something fun for this week!

Positive Affirmation of the Day: My life is fun! (Do this in the mirror.)

Quote of the Day: "Never, ever underestimate the importance of having fun." —Randy Pausch

DAY THIRTY-EIGHT

We Miss All the Shots We Don't Take

HAVE YOU EVER been to a sporting event where the best athlete is just having an off day? In basketball it could be the leading scorer for the team who can't make a shot. In baseball the best hitter keeps swinging and missing. In soccer the top player is missing goal attempts. In football the quarterback is either under or overthrowing every pass. I could go on and on with every sport, but I think you get the point. What happens next has always fascinated me.

Does that player ask the coach to take them out of the game? Does the struggling star stop trying to perform at a high level for the rest of the game? Do they blame the other players around them? The answer to those three questions is: NO, NO, AND NO! The star players do the exact opposite of any of those things. They play harder and keep shooting, swinging, kicking, and throwing for the rest of the game, no matter how painful that performance may have been. They let the boos from the crowd motivate them! *THEY KEEP SHOOTING* and don't take themselves out of the game just because it isn't going well. If anything they get more invested in that particular game. Then they show up early and stay late for the following few practices to ensure it doesn't happen in the next performance. This attitude is what makes them champions. When the going gets tough, they keep going!

Life is the same way; if we give up and stop shooting for our goals just because we have a bad day, week, or even one of those inevitable tough seasons of life, guess what? We won't hit those goals because, just like the All-Star athletes mentioned above, *WE MISS ALL THE SHOTS WE DON'T TAKE!* They don't stop

77

playing; they know it's just a slump, and all athletes go through those. Well, guess what? We all go through those times in life too! So the next time you want to get down and give up just because you get into one of those slumps of life, remember the only way it's going to get better is if you don't give up and keep shooting for your goals. Now keep jumping over any obstacles that get in your way, get out there, and chase your dreams today!

Today's Challenge: Write down the top five reasons you should never give up, and then keep that list somewhere where you'll see it daily.

Positive Affirmation of the Day: I keep going when the going gets tough. I'm a Champion! (Do this in the mirror.)

Quote of the Day: "I've missed more than 9,000 shots in my career. I've lost almost 300 games. 26 times, I've been trusted to take the game-winning shot and missed. I've failed over and over and over again in my life. And that is why I succeed." —Michael Jordan

Day Thirty-Nine

Thoughts Become Things

HAVE YOU EVER had a bad day? Of course you have; we all have! How about a bad week? Once again we all have, right? What about a bad month or even a bad year? Sadly some of you are still shaking your head, and you may even be in the midst of a bad season of life. If that's you I want to give you some hope today! I have good news for you!

You can change this pattern; it's important to remember that *"we become what we think about."* If you constantly think that things will go wrong, guess what? That will happen, and life will throw you what you expect, bad things. However if you expect good days and good things to happen, it works the other way. Guess what? Over time they absolutely will, and you're in store for a much happier life.

Our thoughts and subsequent actions determine whether a day/month/year/ season of our life will be good or bad. *THOUGHTS BECOME THINGS.* Do you want a better, happier life? Think about that then; think about what your life would be like if everything was the way you want it to be; daydream about it, write it down, find pictures of what you want in your life, and put them up around your house so you can see them every day. Your mind is a powerful thing; use it to your advantage!

Do you want a better life? Do you want to be happier? It all starts by looking in the mirror and changing your thoughts. Below are the lyrics from the Michael Jackson song *"Man in the Mirror."* They relate to today's subject; happiness starts by looking at yourself in the mirror and making that change!

I'm starting with the man in the mirror

I'm asking him to change his ways

And no message could've been any clearer
If they want to make the world a better place
Take a look at yourself and then MAKE A CHANGE
MAKE THAT CHANGE TODAY!

Today's Challenge: Look up and listen to the Michael Jackson song "Man in the Mirror." Listen to the words and realize that change starts inside us. Make that change.

Positive Affirmation of the Day: I will be the change I want to see in this world. I become what I think about, and I think positive thoughts! (Do this in the mirror.)

Quote of the Day: "The mind is everything. What you think you become." —Buddha

DAY FORTY

Storms of Life

STORMS ARE SCARY; the damage they can inflict is something to fear. The high winds and lightning can be devastating. However there is always good that comes out of every storm. What is good you ask? Is it the rainbow that comes afterward, the beautiful sun that inevitably shines so bright immediately after the rain, or could it be something beyond what the eye can see, the transformation that takes place in nature?

You see a storm brings so many things that we don't think about consciously. We all know these things, but we are too busy looking at the pretty rainbow and the bright sun in the sky after the rain that we forget the best part of the storm. We forget that storms are necessary for our world and nature to run their course. We don't think about the rainfall, how important it is for any and everything in nature to grow, and how it increases the flow of rivers and streams and helps drag waste away. Storms help balance heat in the oceans and carry nutrients into the sea. They say that even a "hurricane" positively affects the earth, helping to balance global heat, replenish barrier islands and inland plant life, and spread seeds for new growth. All these positive effects and still all we can think about is either the adverse effects and damage a storm may cause or the beauty that comes with rainbows and sunshine after the storm.

Life's storms are no different; let's look at what's going on during the ***STORMS OF LIFE...*** There will be thunder (fear), which will scare us into thinking we can't get through. There will be bright lightning (issues), which will seem impossible during the storm. There will be high wind gusts (outside influences), which will try to knock us down even further and make us believe there is no way out. There will also be rain and lots of it (flooding us with self-doubt),

81

which will try to keep us in the storm longer. Those are the harmful effects of life's storms.

Now let's look at the positive effects. The same thunder, lightning, high wind, and rain that can be damaging can also have healing and restoration powers if we look at them with a positive mindset, which is what this book is all about. Instead of fearing the thunder, what if we welcomed it and said, "I'm going to feel this fear and then move forward anyway?" Rather than succumbing to the lightning, what if we said, "These things happen to everyone. It's just my turn, and I'm going to get through this?" Would we get through the storms of life faster if we blocked those high winds that are telling us to give up or this is too much for us to handle and instead believed in ourselves and God to get through it despite the challenges it's throwing at us faster than we can seem to dodge them? And lastly what if instead of allowing the rain to flood us with a victim mentality, we decided to put up sandbags to protect our minds and dug into positive reading and learning to flood our brains with information that would help us get through the storm? If we look at the storms of life as opportunities to grow, learn, and become stronger, guess what? That's what will happen!

Today's Challenge: Think about your last storm in life, and compare your mindset to the one recommended today. Think about how much faster you could've made it through with a positive attitude and how much better you would've been after the storm.

Positive Affirmation of the Day: I'm strong! I can and will get through the storms in my life. (Do this in the mirror.)

Quote of the Day: "Not all storms come to disrupt your life; some come to clear your path." —Unknown

DAY FORTY-ONE

Live for Today

DO YOU EVER regret anything that you've done or has happened to you in your life? Do you find yourself living on past victories or successes? Do you worry about tomorrow or what the future may bring? Do you focus most of your time on the future? If you're anything like me, the answer to those questions is a resounding YES, YES, YES, and YES! Most of us are so busy thinking about yesterday or tomorrow that we tend to forget the moments we live in right now! Today is the here and now; it's right in front of us, but often we don't live in it because we're too busy celebrating past victories, wallowing in past sorrows and regrets, and worrying about and overplanning for the future (tomorrow). Does this sound familiar? If so I have three words for you: *LIVE FOR TODAY!*

What good does thinking about the wins and losses of the past do for us? If we live on past victories, it's easy to get complacent and not grow. Do you know anyone like this? They're constantly talking about that undefeated season they had their senior year in football or the record they set twenty years ago in the 100-meter dash. I'm not saying that accomplishments like that aren't something to be proud of, because they are; I'm just saying that we can't live only in those moments or let them define who we are now. Then we have those who constantly focus on past mistakes and failures. This thinking can be even worse for us as it makes us feel inferior and like we will never be good enough. I'm not suggesting we forget about our past, it's part of our lives, but rather that we learn from our wins and losses and move forward to the here and now.

Lastly we have the future, and while I believe it's 100% vital to our success always to be setting goals and planning big things for tomorrow and beyond, I also think that too many of us get so focused on tomorrow and the future that we forget how to live for today. We get so caught up in what we "want to have later in life" that we forget to enjoy what we have right now. I love the quote, "I remember the days I prayed for the things I have now." Remember you likely prayed for the life you have now. Enjoy it!

Yesterday is gone, and tomorrow may never come! LIVE FOR TODAY!

Today's Challenge: Write down five things you have in your life that you could've only wished or prayed for five years ago. Then take some time to be happy with where you are right now.

Positive Affirmation of the Day: Today is here right now, and I will enjoy it! (Do this in the mirror.)

Quote of the Day: "Living in the moment means letting go of the past and not waiting for the future. It means living your life consciously, aware that each moment you breathe is a gift." —Oprah Winfrey

Get Back Up

"I GET KNOCKED down, but I get up again; you are never gonna keep me down." The lyrics for the Chumbawamba hit song "Tubthumping" tell us a lot about how to make it through life's challenges. Nothing in those lyrics tells us how to avoid getting knocked down; instead the focus is on the most important part of getting knocked down: to *GET BACK UP AGAIN...* We will all get knocked down in life; that's inevitable. What we do after will make us or, quite frankly, break us!

In life it's not *if* we encounter obstacles, problems, issues, etc., it's *when* and *how often*. Not to say that there is nothing we can do to avoid these things from happening in our lives; most of the pages in this book are full of ways to prevent such things. However life's problems will still find us despite our best efforts to avoid them. If you're anything like me, they show up right before breakthroughs. So while I'm not a fan of negativity in my life, I've learned that it's necessary if I want to be successful. Whether your issues come during moments of strength or weakness, you can and will overcome them with the right attitude. When you fall *GET BACK UP AGAIN!*

Whatever you do don't get discouraged when negative things happen in your life; keep hearing those Chumbawamba lyrics from above in your head. *"I GET KNOCKED DOWN, BUT I GET UP AGAIN; YOU ARE NEVER GONNA KEEP ME DOWN!"* When problems arise remember that opportunity is close behind, so the next time you get knocked down, go ahead and smile or laugh, then get your butt back up again and go after your hopes and dreams. Nothing worth achieving in life is going to come easy. I'm here to tell you, though, the gain is worth the pain. Oh yeah, one more thing for today.

If you don't want to have problems in life, don't do anything at all. But we all know that doing nothing is a problem in and of itself.

Today's Challenge: Look up the song "Tubthumping" by Chumbawamba and listen to the beginning a few times. You'll be glad you did.

Positive Affirmation of the Day: When I get knocked down, I GET BACK UP! (Do this in the mirror.)

Quote of the Day: "The real risk is doing nothing." —Dennis Waitley

Get Moving

HAVE YOU EVER had one of those days where you woke up on the wrong side of the bed and no matter what you did to shake off the funk, you just couldn't? I recently had one of those days; I was in a bad mood all day, and my positive habits didn't feel the same. I wrote in my gratitude journal and still felt ungrateful. I wrote my goals in my goal journal and still felt empty. I did some reading and writing. I even tried making a positive video to post on my social media pages and still couldn't shake that blah feeling. I did everything I could to get my head back straight, and nothing seemed to work. My day was just doomed, or was it?

It was at that point I decided to do a quick workout. I didn't want to, and I certainly didn't think that working out would be what whipped my heart and mind back into shape. I was doing the workout out of habit. I decided six months ago that I would be in the best shape of my life this year, so working out has just become a part of my life. Well, that day working out had a very positive effect on my attitude. Who knew all I had to do that day was get my heart rate up and break a good sweat to get my positive mindset back on track? Not me! So if you're feeling down, *MOVE YOUR BODY! (See day five for some of the mental benefits of a good workout!)*

Working out is good for the body and also super positive for our mindset and mood. Have you ever heard of "runner's high"? It's a real thing, and health-line.com describes it this way. A runner's high is a brief deeply relaxing state of euphoria. Healthline also adds that it occurs after intense or lengthy exercise, and often people who experience a runner's high also report feeling less anxiety and pain immediately after their run.

A "runner's" high is what I experienced that day. It was a fantastic feeling of accomplishment, and I told Tara that whenever I'm feeling down in the future, I'll do my workout early in the day to get my mind back on track. So today's message is simple. Do you want to feel better both physically and mentally? Do you want to avoid having those bad days in life? Do you want to experience that "runner's high"? Then follow this advice. ***Get moving!***

*NOTICE: **Because everyone has a different situation with their health. Please consult a physician for advice on what type of workout is right for you.***

Today's Challenge: Move your body; even a fifteen–thirty-minute brisk walk could change your mood. Try it and see for yourself.

Positive Affirmation of the Day: I'm healthy and have healthy habits. (Do this in the mirror.)

Quote of the Day: "You are one workout away from a good mood." —Anonymous

Attitude Is Everything

HAVE YOU EVER noticed that no matter what the task or challenge, when you go into it with a positive outlook and a good attitude, it seems much easier to get it done? Have you noticed the exact opposite is also true? When we go into a situation already defeated and tell ourselves how bad it will be, it usually is! So the mindset we take into every day of our lives does matter. *ATTITUDE IS EVERYTHING!*

We're all human, so naturally we dread things in our lives. How about being late, traffic jams, sitting next to a talker on an airplane, long business meetings, mandatory overtime, the dentist or doctor, busy shopping malls, getting put on hold, the BMV, or packing for a vacation, the list could go on and on, but you get the point. These are some pretty stressful situations that we all deal with in our lives. How is your attitude when things like this happen? If you're anything like me, you're not excited about any of the above scenarios.

I'm not suggesting that a positive attitude will make these situations desirable, but since these things are just part of life, if we go into them with a good mindset, they will pass faster and be much easier to deal with. I like to look at it this way, "This too shall pass," and I'll be back doing something I love again soon.

"Life is 10% what happens to you and 90% how you react to it."
—*Charles R. Swindoll*

The quote above sums up today's message; we'll all deal with unpleasant days and situations, and how we react to those days will determine what type of life we have. Do you want to be happy? It starts with understanding that *ATTITUDE IS*

EVERYTHING! A positive attitude doesn't make your life perfect, but it will make your life much better than the alternative of having a negative outlook. If you're looking for perfection, life will be challenging, but I have great news: happiness is possible without life being perfect. It starts with a positive attitude and mindset.

Today's Challenge: Reread the second paragraph above, and try to come up with one positive thing that could come out of each stressful scenario listed. For example I was running late, but I may have avoided an accident. (See that's positive.)

Positive Affirmation of the Day: I have an outstanding attitude, my happiness is my choice, and I'm happy today. (Do this in the mirror.)

Quote of the Day: "If you are positive, you'll see opportunities instead of obstacles." —Confucius

DAY FORTY-FIVE

Crawl, Walk, Then Run

CAN A NEWBORN baby run, walk, or even crawl? That's a silly question. Of course a newborn can't do those things. Newborns aren't strong enough to lift their heads, let alone start crawling. We must do everything for them until they learn how to become mobile! Before we know it, they're rolling over, sitting up, then crawling, and sometime later we find them standing on their own two feet. It's then and only then, after months and months of trying and failing, that they are finally strong enough to walk and then run! The moral of today's message is that just like a newborn baby, we must constantly learn new things and get stronger to become high achievers or experts in any area of our lives. It's important to remember that we have to *CRAWL, WALK, THEN RUN!*

Many times in life, we expect to jump right into new things and be good at them, and unfortunately that's just not how it works. We must be willing to start at the bottom and be amateur first. To get better we must be ready to study and practice. Over time with patience, dedication, and a lot of blood, sweat, and tears, we can become experts or professionals at just about anything we desire. We have to be willing to crawl before we walk and walk before we run, but make no mistake, we can be "running" in just about anything when we put in the time and effort necessary to learn and perfect it!

So many of us want to get better at our jobs, earn promotions, have better friendships and relationships with loved ones, grow closer to God, or be better people in general… I've got good news, all of these things can become our reality if we *CRAWL, WALK, THEN RUN* in that order! Always be willing to put the time and effort into making your life the best it can be. I know I say this a lot, but it's true. You'll thank yourself later!

Today's Challenge: Consider one thing you want to learn or improve on, then intentionally do something today that will get you closer to making it a reality.

Positive Affirmation of the Day: I'm willing to do whatever it takes to better myself. (Do this in the mirror.)

Quote of the Day: "In life, we must first learn to crawl, then stand, then walk, then run, and only then, fly. We cannot crawl into flying." —RVM

DAY FORTY-SIX

Balance

DO YOU WANT more out of life? Of course you do; we all do! What if I told you that the life of your dreams is possible? Not only is it possible, but it's highly likely when you develop good positive habits. We all have habits; the question we need to ask ourselves is, are they helping us to achieve the life we truly desire or are they keeping us stuck right where we are now? Only you can answer that question for your life. Today I'm asking you to do a little self-reflection and ask yourself these tough questions:

Do I have good or bad habits in the following areas of my life?

- Mental health / Emotional well-being
- Physical health
- Personal growth
- Spiritual life
- Family
- Career/Job
- Relationships/Friendships
- Financial

I understand this can be overwhelming. Be careful not to beat yourself up! What we are trying to develop is *BALANCE*, not perfection! The happiest people I've ever met have a healthy balance of these things in their lives. No one is perfect; don't expect perfection; improve in each area over time. Progress doesn't happen overnight; it takes time. Be patient!

In the areas you've already developed good habits, keep those going. If you've developed bad habits or don't have any at all, start working on making small changes each day. You'll be surprised how fast you'll start to see results. The old analogy is "the grass isn't greener on the other side of the fence." Sometimes the grass is greener, but it's because it is watered and taken care of as it should be. If we begin to work on the areas where we need improvement, our grass will look just as green in no time! What are you waiting for? Get out there and live the life of your dreams!

Today's Challenge: Answer the questions above, then start working on the areas you may be weak in.

Positive Affirmation of the Day: I'm living the life of my dreams! (Do this in the mirror.)

Quote of the Day: "Balance is not something you find, it's something you create." —Jana Kingsford

Under Promise, then Overdeliver

HAVE YOU EVER been in a situation where a salesperson, job recruiter, or friend made promises that seemed "too good to be true"? I call this overpromising, and unfortunately it's a common practice in the world we live in today. The biggest problem with overpromising is that it almost always leads to underdelivering. If we flip that and under promise and then overdeliver, we would be much better off. In doing so we can do what we say we will and go the extra mile. That is how you build an excellent reputation. Are you starting to catch my drift? Do you want to be respected both personally and professionally? Start living by this principle in everything you do. ***UNDER PROMISE AND THEN OVERDELIVER!***

The good news is that many people do it this way. They are likely the people you enjoy being around the most and love doing business with.

Overpromising has become common because people are trying to compete to a fault. I want the truth, good or bad, and I don't want to be lied to for someone to gain my friendship or business. In almost every case where we are overpromised and underdelivered, we will tell other people about it, and that's not good for the person or business. On the other hand, when a person ends up overdelivering because they were smart enough not to overpromise, we tell people about that too, which is very good for that person!

Because you are the type of person that bought and is reading a book like this one, I'm confident that you're already living your life as an over deliverer. But in case you aren't, I hope the points I've made in today's message will sway you to this side of the fence.

Today's Challenge: Think about the last time someone overpromised and then underdelivered to you. How did that make you feel? Remember that feeling and be an over-deliverer from now on.

Positive Affirmation of the Day: My promises are true. I have integrity and overdeliver! (Do this in the mirror.)

Quote of the Day: "Formula for success: under promise and over deliver." —Tom Peters

Take Action

We've covered so much in the first forty-seven days of our mindset challenge, from positive affirmations to setting goals, developing a plan to achieving those goals, gratitude, faith, happiness, and how and why to have a never-give-up attitude. We've also gone over how positive daily habits are vital to our success, how to build self-esteem, how and why to treat others how we'd like them to treat us, and so much more. Today we will cover a topic that will help us put what we've learned to good use. It's time to *TAKE ACTION!*

To benefit from the lessons in this book, we must first understand that what we've learned can only do us good when we apply it. We can read and learn over and over about how to improve our lives and mindset, but we will only see positive results after we take action. You may wonder how I know you want these things; it's pretty simple. You would only make it this far in the book if you were serious about changing your life and developing a new and improved positive mindset. So congrats on making it this far. I'm confident that your perspective is already better than on day one. Taking action today and beyond on everything you're learning will determine just how deep the transformation of your mind will go!

I firmly believe that knowledge without action is meaningless. Knowing what to do and not doing it is insane. Below is Albert Einstein's definition of insanity; it pertains to today's topic.

Insanity: "Doing the same thing over and over and expecting different results."
—Albert Einstein

I challenge you not only to learn the material, but also to put it into action. I can promise you one thing: when you do you'll live a life full of joy and happiness. Your days will be more productive and full of joy and happiness. I don't know about you, but that's the kind of life I wanted when I set out on my new mindset mission many years ago! I'm happy to report that everything in this book works; it's all tried and true by yours truly on my journey! However it only works if you do, so *TAKE ACTION TODAY!*

Today's Challenge: Pick one area you've learned about in this book and take that action.

Positive Affirmation of the Day: I will take action today to live the life of my dreams. (Do this in the mirror.)

Quote of the Day: "The only impossible journey is the one you never begin." —Tony Robbins

DAY FORTY-NINE

See Your Worth

WHO ARE YOU? What do you stand for? What kind of morals and values do you have? Are you the kind of person you would enjoy being friends with? Are you a good spouse / significant other? A good parent or grandparent? How about in your work life? Are you a good coworker? Are you a manager, leader, or owner in your career? If so would you want to work under your leadership? *SEE YOUR WORTH!* The first step is to love yourself; once you do it will be much easier for the people around you to love you.

Ask yourself these two questions. First do you love yourself? Second do the people around you look up to, love, and respect you?

I realize these are tough questions to answer, but I also know that we need to do a self-assessment occasionally to grow. That's all I'm asking you to do today. Give yourself a report card, grade yourself in the following areas in an A–F format, and be honest; that's the only way this exercise will help you. You'll be the only one to see it! If you have an A or a B in an area, keep doing what you're doing. If it's a C or below, that's ok too; the good news is this will help expose the areas you may be weak in! Then develop some healthy habits in those areas to get better! Let's not beat ourselves up; this is all about self-improvement! I wrote this book to help people like YOU and me improve our mindset and live better, happier lives. *SEE YOUR WORTH!*

Grade yourself in the following areas:

- Relationship with spouse / significant other:
- Family and friends:
- Career/Job:

- Morals and values:
- Spiritual life:
- Mental health:
- Physical health:
- Personal growth:
- Finances:

Now the only thing left to do is pat yourself on the back for the areas you graded yourself high on! Next plan to develop better habits in the areas where you graded yourself lower. Start with baby steps, and remember small changes over time lead to true transformation.

Today's Challenge: Do today's exercise and then write out a few things you will start doing effective immediately to get some of the grades up.

Positive Affirmation of the Day: I love myself and my life; I'm getting better every day. (Do this in the mirror.)

Quote of the Day: "Love yourself first, and everything else falls into line. You really have to love yourself to get anything done in this world." —Lucille Ball

DAY FIFTY

Love with All Your Heart

LOVE IS BEAUTIFUL, whether from family, friends, or an actual romantic relationship. It feels good to love and to be loved. No feeling compares to knowing someone truly loves us, can't live without us, and would do anything for us. Conversely it feels so good to give love in those same ways. The Bible says in 1 Corinthians 13:4, "Love is patient, love is kind, it does not envy, it does not boast, it is not proud." That appeals to me!

It's possible you didn't grow up in a loving and affectionate home or your spouse / significant other doesn't show you the kind of love I'm describing here. In that case you may find it uncomfortable to express your love toward people outwardly. I understand, but I want you to consider giving as much love as possible despite what you're getting or how uncomfortable it makes you feel. If you've read this book up to this point, you already realize that *"we become what we think about"* and that *"the power of positive thinking"* works in our lives. So whether you have nurtured loving relationships at the moment or not, read the following two paragraphs with an open mind and then pour out as much love as you possibly can into the relationships that you have in your life. Do you want to feel loved? You must first ***LOVE WITH ALL YOUR HEART!***

According to canopyhealth.com (article on March 11, 2017, titled: How Does Love Affect Our Physical Health?) love affects not only our physical health, but also our mental wellbeing. I think most of the physical benefits of a sexual relationship go without saying, but I'll share a few with you. Making love can lower blood pressure, reduce stress, improve sleep, and boost the immune system. So falling in love and being sexually involved in and of itself is good for our physical health. Sex is good for us!

Now the mental benefits that a loving relationship has on us. Studies show that romantic, family, friendship, or other types of love can lead to higher self-esteem, increased sense of self-worth, and improved self-confidence. Loving relationships can reduce anxiety and worry and can lower the risk of depression and other forms of mental illness. So love with all your heart today; it's good for your health!

Today's Challenge: Tell someone you love them and show someone you love them!

Positive Affirmation of the Day: I will love with all my heart today! (Do this in the mirror.)

Quote of the Day: "Love has nothing to do with what you are expecting to get—only with what you are expecting to give—which is everything." —Katharine Hepburn

DAY FIFTY-ONE

Success

ACCORDING TO THE *Merriam-Webster* dictionary, success is *"a degree of measure, a favorable or desired outcome, also the attainment of wealth, favor, or eminence."* An old friend of mine used to jokingly define success as "making more money than his wife could spend." The funny part of him saying that is that he did indeed make and save more money than she could spend. Maybe there was something phycological about him saying it that brought it into existence. We do become what we think about. His definition of success had to do with how much money he could accumulate; yours may be completely different. **What is success?** Every one of us will have a different definition of what success means to us. What does success mean to you?

Many areas of life are meaningful. From physical and mental health, personal growth, spiritual life, family, career, and relationships to financial wellbeing. While all of these are at least somewhat important to us, each of us has an area or two that stands out as the most important. Our definition of success is likely to be heavily weighed by how we are doing in these areas that we prioritize as most important.

So today I'm asking you to look hard at your priorities and determine your definition of success. There is no wrong answer to what success looks like to you; remember it will be your life's definition. Be creative, use your imagination, and think about what would make you the happiest; usually if you can figure out what will make you excited and passionate, you're on the right track to finding your definition of success.

What are you waiting for? Start brainstorming today. The sooner you figure this out, the sooner you can start setting new goals, planning, and taking action toward the successful life you want and deserve.

Today's Challenge: Take some time to brainstorm and write down some of the things that are important to you and would make you the happiest.

Positive Affirmation of the Day: I can, I will, I am a successful person! (Do this in the mirror.)

Quote of the Day: "The key to success is to start before you are ready." —Marie Forleo

DAY FIFTY-TWO

The Best Things
in Life Are…

FILL IN THE blank. The best things in life are _____. We've all heard the old saying that *"the best things in life are free,"* right? Well, do you agree with that? It's ok if you do, but it's also ok if you don't. You see the best things in life to me will be completely different from the best things in life to you. We all have those things we just can't or don't want to live without. **THE BEST THINGS!**

If you find yourself on the side of the fence that says the best things in life are free, you're not alone by any means. Let's discuss the free things that most of us wouldn't want to live without. Here we go: hugs, kisses, love, smiles, friends, family, sleep, good health, laughter, the sun, the moon, stars, and all other things Mother Nature gives us to look at. That is a pretty good list.

Maybe you are on the other side that says nope, I want the things in life that money can buy. So let's look at the things that cost us our time, hard work, effort, and money to obtain. How about a house, car or truck, vacation, remodel of your home, wardrobe, a lake house and boat, cash in the bank, and investments, how about going to concerts or plays, sporting events, this list could go on and on, but you get the point. That is also a good list.

I understand if you fall into either category. We can all agree that the things listed in the "free" category are necessities, and we all desire to have them. I'd also like to think that if you care enough about your quality of life to purchase a book like this one, you'll also be the type of person that wants most, if not all, of the things listed in the "things that cost" category as well. Could the best things in life be *ALL OF THE ABOVE?* A mix of the things money can and can't buy is how most of us will find true happiness. A balance of both is likely the ticket to a joy-filled life.

I don't know anyone truly happy who doesn't have a mix of the things money can and can't buy. So enjoy those free things of life, as we can't live happily without them; however set your goals high and work on obtaining some things money can buy. I know you want and deserve both!

Today's Challenge: Make a list of three things that money can't buy and then three things money can buy that you genuinely believe are the best things for you to live a joy-filled life.

Positive Affirmation of the Day: I'm living the life of my dreams. (Do this in the mirror.)

Quote of the Day: "The best things in life are often waiting for you at the exit ramp of your comfort zone." —Karen Salmansohn

Work Hard...Play Harder

SINCE YOU ARE reading this book, I will go on a limb and say you're a motivated individual already and have a good work ethic. If I'm right congratulations, you've already got half of today's message under control.

If you need help with a good work ethic, I'll give you a couple of tidbits that should help. First make sure you're passionate about your work; when you have a deep passion for what you do, it makes it easier to show up and do it day in and day out. Second talk positively about your career/job and coworkers. We believe what we tell ourselves, and the fastest way to lose motivation and start slacking on the job is to profess negatively about it. Stay positive! Once again most people reading books like this one are self-motivated, so you have already mastered the *WORK-HARD* part of today's message. If so congrats; if not take the two tips I gave to heart and make some positive changes to develop better work habits.

Now for the second half of today's message, the fun part, but all too often, it needs to be practiced more by highly motivated people with good work ethics. You see the *PLAY-HARDER* part of this is easier said than done for us workaholics of the world. We get so caught up in the work that we sometimes forget to reward ourselves. Does this sound familiar to you? Is this you or someone you know? The play-harder side is where balance comes into play (see day forty-six). To maintain a positive attitude in the long run—and believe me if you want to stay passionate, motivated, and keep working long hours—you will need some downtime to do things you love. PLAY HARD! Go on vacations, to concerts, ball games, plays, your kid's sporting events, movies, date nights, etc.

I call this recharging our mental battery, and it's vital so we can keep our motivation high and avoid the dreaded burnout, which is inevitable if we don't take some "me time."

So **WORK HARD** for sure, but...*PLAY HARDER!*

Today's Challenge: Think about your life and write down the last thing you did to recharge your battery for fun. How did this make you feel?

Positive Affirmation of the Day: I work hard to play harder! (Do this in the mirror.)

Quote of the Day: "When you play, play hard; when you work, don't play at all."
—Theodore Roosevelt

Day Fifty-Four

Sometimes You Win... Sometimes You Learn

I WANT TO challenge you to think about the wins and losses you've had. What is the most significant accomplishment you've ever had? What is your biggest failure? Those two questions should get you thinking. I know that you've had plenty of both. How do I know this, you ask? Because you are a human being, winning and losing are just facts of life. You see sometimes you win, and sometimes you lose. Today I want to flip the script, though, and instead say: *SOMETIMES YOU WIN...SOMETIMES YOU LEARN!*

Winning in life is a fantastic feeling for sure. Just think about the last time your team won a big game, you won an award, achieved a goal, got a promotion, or any other happy moment you've had. There is no feeling like the feeling of success; it gives us energy, motivation, inspiration, and just about every other good emotion. I'm so thankful for all my wins; I'm sure you're grateful for yours too!

Losing, however, brings an entirely different set of emotions with it. Think of the last time your team lost a big game, you didn't win the award you were striving so hard to earn, you lost your job or got demoted, or any other time in your life you failed at anything. Those moments and events bring disappointment, sadness, anger, shame, and many other emotions we don't want. So what do we do to flip that script in these situations? We learn from failure, grow from it, and improve so that the next time we put ourselves in a better position to win. Never quit; learn from losses and failures and move on to the next attempt! Like the great Zig Ziglar used to say, "Failure is an event, not a person."

Did you know that Sir James Dyson had over 5,000 failed prototypes over fifteen years before creating the bagless vacuum cleaner we all know as a "Dyson"? At the time of this writing, he has a net worth of over $4.5 billion. I'll bet he's glad he kept learning rather than quitting because of all those failed attempts. Never give up; keep learning and looking for the lesson in each failure.

Today's Challenge: Write down what you believe to be your most significant accomplishment ever, then think about all the times you had to try and fail to hit that win. This little exercise will give you all the reasons you need to keep learning from your losses in life.

Positive Affirmation of the Day: I NEVER GIVE UP, I NEVER QUIT, and I LEARN FROM FAILURE. (Do this in the mirror.)

Quote of the Day: "The only real mistake is the one from which we learn nothing." —Henry Ford

DAY FIFTY-FIVE

Self-Love

A FEW DAYS ago (day fifty), our topic was "love with all your heart." We discussed the feeling of loving and being loved by others and what that can do for us physically and mentally. As we learned the effects are healthy for the body and mind. Today let's talk about another important form of love. *SELF-LOVE!!*

You may be thinking, isn't that kind of love selfish? Not at all! If we want to earn the love and respect of others, we must first learn to love and respect ourselves. I'm not talking about having an unhealthy love of ourselves; there is a fine line between loving and respecting yourself and being downright arrogant and conceited. Those two traits make it harder for people to love us and will have the opposite effect and push people away. However having confidence in yourself, high self-esteem, and knowing that you are a good person and care about yourself and your loved ones makes it much easier for people to love you back.

Think about the people you love the most in your life; I mean those friends, coworkers, and family members you love to be around and can't get enough of. Do they put off good vibes? Are they positive? Are they fun to be around? I already know the answers to those three questions, YES, YES, and YES! How do I know that? People who are confident yet not arrogant, positive yet not fake, and like to have fun are people everyone wants to associate with as often as possible. What else do these friends, coworkers, and family members share? If you guessed they have a healthy self-image and love and respect who they are, you got it right!

So do you want to be the kind of person who is easy to love and whom others want to spend more time with? Of course you do; we all do.

Take some time to think about yourself and your life up to this point. Think about any and everything that you've ever done that is good. Then pat yourself on the back and say, "I love myself, I respect myself, I'm a good person, and people love me too." Then tell yourself that every day! Over time you'll believe more in yourself and find that healthy self-love we all deserve. It may take a little time to buy into this, but when you do, you'll find that the relationships in your life will drastically improve. You'll become that person everyone else loves and wants to be around.

Today's Challenge: Think of two people in your life who you believe already have the SELF-LOVE concept down. Then write down a few of the traits they have that you like. Now start working on those traits in your own life.

Positive Affirmation of the Day: I love myself; I'm a good person! (Do this in the mirror.)

Quote of the Day: "How you love yourself is how you teach others to love you." —Rupi Kaur

Show up Prepared

I'M A BIG college basketball fan, so I love the time of year known as March Madness! I can't help but notice that some teams are prepared and ready to play, while others show up unprepared and look lethargic. Guess who wins those games almost every time? That's right, the teams that *SHOW UP PREPARED!!!*

The National Collegiate Athletics Association (NCAA) tournament is a lot like the game of life, and those who show up the most prepared are the ones who will end up being victorious more times than not. Sometimes people will say, "That team just got lucky to win," or, "He or she just got lucky getting that promotion." Oprah Winfrey and Zig Ziglar have both said, "Luck is what happens when PREPARATION meets OPPORTUNITY."

So the more prepared you are, the luckier you appear. But we all know that luck has nothing to do with it. How do teams win the big games? How do people get promotions? How and why do people or companies get big deals in the business world? While there are many different reasons, I can tell you with 100% certainty that one of the keys is that those teams and individuals came to the game of life prepared to win, get promoted, or get that business deal. They didn't just show up expecting something big to happen.

Preparation will be different for all of us; it's also different for every scenario or situation. A basketball team, for example, would prepare for a big game by watching videos of the opponent, practicing, and conditioning. A person would prepare for a promotion by showing up on time to work each day, completing all tasks given to them by their superiors in a timely and professional manner, and of course by going the extra mile. That never hurts! Lastly a person, sales team, or company would prepare to get a business deal by studying the person or company they are trying to sell to and finding a way to fulfill a need or solve a problem that person or company may have. In all these cases, preparation is one of the biggest keys to success!

Do you want to wander through your life and take what life throws at you? Or do you want to take the extra time, put the extra effort into preparation, and live the life of your dreams? Only you can answer that question.

Today's Challenge: Think about the last big win you had in life, and reflect on the preparation it took beforehand.

Positive Affirmation of the Day: I'm willing to do whatever it takes to win. (Do this in the mirror.)

Quote of the Day: "Failing to prepare is preparing to fail." —John Wooden

Day Fifty-Seven

Be the Change You Want to See

Have you ever thought and wished this world was different and hoped that someone would do something to make it better? Have you ever thought things would be much better if others would change, pull their weight, or do more? One last question. Have you ever thought about making those changes, pulling your weight, and being that change you want to see in our world? *BE THE CHANGE YOU WANT TO SEE!*

You may be probably thinking, what could someone like me do to change the world? I'm here to tell you that change starts with you and me and happens one person and one day at a time. If we want to see a better world for future generations, change starts with each of us. And, yes, each one of us can make a difference. Have you ever heard the "starfish story"?

The Starfish Story, by Loren Eiseley:

One day, a man was walking along the beach when he noticed a boy picking something up and gently throwing it into the ocean. Approaching the boy, he asked, "What are you doing?"

The boy replied, "Throwing starfish back into the ocean. The surf is up and the tide is going out. If I don't throw them back, they'll die."

"Son," the man said, "don't you realize there are miles and miles of beach and hundreds of starfish? You can't make a difference!"

After listening politely, the boy bent down, picked up another starfish, and threw it back into the surf. Then, smiling at the man, he said." I made a difference for that one."

The moral of that little story is that any one of us can make a difference in this world. Do you want people to be more likable? Be nice! Do you want others to smile more? Smile at everyone you see! Do you want better teaching in our schools? Show up to the school board meetings! Do you want your child to have a better coach in sports? Start coaching! Do you want more people to trust in God? Tell people about your faith! Do you want _____? Fill in the blank with whatever you want to see, and then take it upon yourself to do something about it! It starts with one; let that be you!

Today's Challenge: Think of one change you'd like to see in your community or the world, and then take one action step to help!

Positive Affirmation of the Day: I will be the change I want to see in this world. (Do this in the mirror.)

Quote of the Day: "Be the change you wish to see in the world." —Mahatma Gandhi

DAY FIFTY-EIGHT

Diet Is Key

WE'VE ALL HEARD the old saying, "Garbage in, garbage out." Never is that truer than when talking about our diet and nutrition. Zig Ziglar, a world-renowned sales trainer and motivational speaker, used to get this point across to his audiences by asking them if anyone in the crowd owned a million-dollar racehorse. Of course none of them ever owned one, but what he said next got their attention. He'd say, "If you did own one, would you feed it junk food and allow it to drink alcohol or soda and smoke cigarettes the night before a race?" While that was a silly question, as no one would ever do that to a million-dollar racehorse, let alone the family dog or cat, it made the audience think about what they were eating and drinking themselves. So what are you eating and drinking? *DIET IS KEY!*

Zig would remind the people in attendance that we can't be constantly putting junk into our bodies and expect to be able to perform at a high level. It was always funny to hear him use that analogy, but at the same time, it was eye-opening as it made us think about how we are abusing our bodies and then expecting good performance out of them.

Look at this excerpt from the Sutter Health article titled (Eating Well for Mental Health) From a young age, we're taught that eating well helps us look and feel our physical best. What we're not always told is that good nutrition significantly affects our mental health too. A healthy, well-balanced diet can help us think clearly and feel more alert. It can also improve concentration and attention span. Conversely, an inadequate diet can lead to fatigue, impaired decision-making and can slow down reaction time. In fact, a poor diet can actually aggravate and may even lead to stress and depression.

So diet and nutrition are crucial to us in our journey to develop a more positive mindset. The good news is that we can improve one snack, one meal, and one day at a time. Positive change happens one moment at a time, so stay the course and know that you can do it! Cheers to our healthier future together!

Today's Challenge: Choose something healthy for one of your snacks or meals today. Then do it again tomorrow, and so on.

Positive Affirmation of the Day: I eat healthy foods. I'm healthy! (Do this in the mirror.)

Quote of the day: "The act of nutrition has been proven in research to have a direct correlation with the improvement of mental health." —Eva Selhub (MD at Harvard University)

DAY FIFTY-NINE

Groundhog Day

HAVE YOU EVER seen the movie *Groundhog Day*? It's about a weatherman who finds himself living the same day over and over again. Do you ever feel like you wake up and live the same day, week, month, or year on repeat? If so you're not alone! I used to feel that way too, and it felt like the same old day lived over and over again. Unless you're extraordinarily analytical or structure oriented, this type of life tends to get boring and can even start to feel negative. So what can we do to break the cycle, transform our lives, and start living the life of our dreams?

In the first fifty-eight days of this book, you'll find a lot of positive daily habits that, if you started doing them, would make the same life feel different. I can help you break this cycle by sharing what I did myself to make positive changes. You see it's not always what we do that makes life feel so repetitive; our perception, attitude, and mindset about what we do make it feel that way. Our lives will always be routine; changing our daily habits can help make life more exciting and fun!

So here goes! Start doing positive affirmations (day two) every morning. Say things to yourself in the mirror like *"I love my life," "I'm having fun today," "I love my job," "I love my life,"* etc. Next pray or meditate often. Thank God for everything He has given you, then ask for help in any areas of your life you need it. If you're not a person of faith, then meditate, think about the things I mentioned, and envision your life as more fun, exciting, and enjoyable. Mindset is everything when it comes down to how we feel about our lives. If we look for and focus on the good, fun, and exciting times of our lives, our perception of life changes.

Set some goals (days twenty-eight and twenty-nine). Goals give us something to shoot for; I can't even imagine not having any goals written down. That would be boring to me. Look at them often; this will keep you excited about reaching them. Zig Ziglar used to say, "Don't be a wandering generality, be a meaningful specific." He was referring to life without goals compared to life with goals.

Lastly use a gratitude journal daily (day thirty-one). At the beginning or end of each day, pull the journal out and write down five–ten things you are thankful for. This exercise does two things for me. First it helps me realize how good my life is. Second it gets me thinking positively all day and actually looking for the good rather than the bad. We all have bad things going on; it's all about where we choose to focus. I love this quote by Tony Robbins, "Where focus goes, energy flows." Where is your focus? Do you want life to be more fun and exciting? Change your habits, change your mindset, and your life will follow.

Today's Challenge: Do something today you've always wanted to do but never have.

Positive Affirmation of the Day: I love my life. (Do this in the mirror.)

Quote of the Day: "Once your mindset changes, everything on the outside will change along with it." —Steve Maraboli

Day Sixty

What-If Thinking

THE MIND IS so powerful; it's crazy how it never stops thinking from the second we wake up until we fall asleep each night. Our mind is the most complex thing about us as human beings; it controls everything we do, both consciously and subconsciously. The subconscious mind is the part that takes care of our physical bodily functions, things like breathing, digestion, and everything else that keeps us alive. The subconscious takes care of them.

The conscious mind, however, is much different; this part of our mind is responsible for rationalizing, paying attention, logical thinking, and reasoning. In other words we have complete control over this part of the mind. You may be wondering why the topic for today is *"WHAT-IF THINKING"* and I'm writing about the brain. It's simple; I want to help you control *"what if"* thinking by using your conscious mind.

If you are someone who has ever suffered from anxiety or depression, then today's topic is especially for you. Most people with anxiety or depression struggle with their *"what if"* thinking. Even if you've never dealt with either of those ailments, I'm sure you've occasionally had some negative *"what if"* thinking. So here is how we can change that.

The words that fill the blank behind "what if _____" can either build us up or destroy us; the good news is, it's 100% within our control. Remember what the conscious mind can do? That's right; it controls our logical thinking and reasoning. Whenever you say *"what if"* and follow it up with something you don't want to happen, you're calling something you are afraid of or don't want right into your life. The good news is, this works the other way too, so the next time you follow your *"what if"* with something you don't want or are afraid of happening, I want you to put your conscious mind to work and *"change that channel"* in your mind from something negative to something positive!

You must catch yourself thinking negative thoughts and immediately give yourself a mental reprimand and change that thought to something positive that you want to happen in your life. Is this easy at first? Nope! Is it easy after you train your mind? Yes, very! Once again developing a positive mindset, which is the goal of this ninety-day challenge, takes time and work and can be challenging. But it's worth it!

Today's Challenge: Catch yourself the next time you have a "what if" moment! Change the negative thought to a positive one immediately!

Positive Affirmation of the Day: What if today is AWESOME? (Do this in the mirror.)

Quote of the Day: "You were born with the greatest weapon in all of nature—the rational, conscious mind." —Robert Greene

Day Sixty-One

Respond

WITH THE INVENTION of the internet and now social media running rampant in our world, never has there been more opportunity for the "haters" to show their lack of class to the rest of us. I'm sure you've dealt with a hater or two. So what is the best way to handle "haters" in our lives and remain upbeat, not letting them affect our journey toward a positive mindset? The best advice I can give you is to let them hate and ignore them. However in many cases, it's more complicated! In these cases I advise you not to react; instead *RESPOND!*

Unfortunately we can't control how other people think and act. However we can control whether we react or respond to the situation. Sometimes we can't ignore a hater or a hateful issue and must decide whether to react or respond. Allow me to explain.

There is a difference between reacting and responding. Reacting is usually a "knee jerk" and happens immediately without any thought. In most cases reacting makes the situation worse and leads to more pain. We've all done this, and we all know how this ends. In this case no one wins, and I want you to be the winner!

The other choice is to wait a while, think about it, sleep on it, then if we still feel it's important to respond, do so with tact and professionalism. Come at the hater with facts and a solid argument about why what they said or did was wrong or insensitive. This approach keeps your integrity intact and makes the hater look and feel foolish. *(Which is what they are.)* Responding is where you win; you be the bigger person and realize they can't truly hurt you without your permission.

Responding rather than reacting gets easier with time; it's just like all the other changes discussed in this book in our quest to develop a positive mindset.

There will undoubtedly be some pain before we gain, but the pain is temporary and worth it!

Lastly when haters notice this change in us, they will find someone else to pick on! They are cowards looking for someone to debate or argue with, so when you stop giving them the reaction they thrive on and are looking for, they will go elsewhere!

Today's Challenge: Live this out the next chance you get. Either ignore the hater or respond after some thought, then watch as they find someone else to pick on.

Positive Affirmation of the Day: I am making positive changes in my life. (Do this in the mirror.)

Quote of the Day: "The best way to counter-attack a hater is to make it blatantly obvious that their attack has had no impact on you." —Tim Ferriss

DAY SIXTY-TWO

Focus on Your Blessings

WITH ALL THE crazy things happening today and the hustle that comes with modern-day life, it's easy to get overwhelmed in this fast-paced life. Stress isn't healthy for us physically or mentally; it affects our bodies, thoughts, feelings, and behavior. According to Mayo Clinic, stress that's left unchecked can contribute to various health problems, such as high blood pressure, heart disease, obesity, and diabetes. So let's get our mindset to the point where we can overcome that stress by focusing on how we are blessed! *FOCUS ON YOUR BLESSINGS!*

Unfortunately stress is a normal part of life. Stress stems from our families, friends, health issues, careers, spiritual lives, divorce, the death of a loved one, finances, and depression or anxiety, to name a few! It's easy to understand why people get so stressed; life is hard. So if you are having issues with any of the above, I want you to pay close attention to *"the rest of the story."*

Now it's time to discuss the kryptonite of stress: our blessings! If you're unfamiliar with kryptonite, the *Oxford Languages dictionary defines it* as something that can seriously weaken or harm a particular person or thing. That's precisely what our blessings will do to stress; they will break it down and loosen its grasp on our lives. It's hard to stay stressed when you focus on all the beautiful things in your life. Yes, I'm telling you that the best way to combat stress is to think about your blessings when you first awaken, at breakfast, at work, during lunch, on your drive home, when you sit down to dinner, and when you go to bed. All of the above are blessings in and of themselves. *(Waking up, breakfast, lunch, our jobs, our vehicle or mode of transportation, dinner, our bed to sleep in.)* I just gave you seven blessings without even getting into your personal lives. If you're a believer, thank God for these blessings too!

How many blessings do you have in your life right now? Take a minute to write some down. For example spouse, kids/family, friends, church, car, wardrobe, phone, etc. From now on anytime you start to feel stressed, remember these blessings are the kryptonite that can fight that stress. When stress rears its ugly head, start writing down all of the blessings you have at that moment and read them repeatedly to remind yourself that you're ***too blessed to be stressed!***

Today's Challenge: Write down ten blessings you currently have. Keep that list nearby, and look at it when you feel stressed.

Positive Affirmation of the Day: I am blessed; I focus on the good things I have in my life. (Do this in the mirror.)

Quote of the Day: "When I started counting my blessings, my whole life turned around." —Willie Nelson

First Time for Everything

From the time we are born until the day we die, everything we do will eventually have the last time. It's often sweet. An example would be graduation; this is a happy time in our lives. Other times the last time is sorrowful, like when we see a loved one for the last time before they pass away. But rest assured, happy or sad, there is indeed a last time for everything.

What if we flipped that around and started to think about the exact opposite of the last time? What if we consciously look back at our lives and remember the first times for everything? Looking at our lives with this perspective will help us live a life of gratitude. Here are a few examples of how this way of thinking can help us develop and maintain the positive mindset we all desire.

Are you having difficulty with a child? Think back and remember the first time you set eyes on that child and how much love you had in your heart. Doing this will help, I promise!

Are you struggling with your relationship? Remember that first date? The first kiss? The first time you said I love you? Will this help you look at your relationship differently? I bet it will!

Is your job getting boring? Do your coworkers annoy you? Think about your first interview to get this job and your first day there. I'll bet those are happy memories. Remember it's the same job as it was that day! It's your perspective that's changed.

Are you having a tough time with _____? You fill in the blank, then think about the first time with that person, place, or thing. I'll bet you felt different the first time than you do now, and at least in some cases, you can get that feeling back again if you just put in some effort and remember how you felt about it in the beginning.

The first time for many things that now make us unhappy was likely a happy time. It's after we do that same thing or spend time with that same person over and over that it can become mundane, dull, or in some cases even toxic. But it's important to remember that at one time, that same person, place, or thing brought us great joy. Looking back and reminiscing about the first time we were with that person, went to that place, or did that thing that is now bringing us unhappiness can help us understand that it may have been us that changed! Our perspective does become our reality, and sometimes we have to look back and change that perspective!

Today's Challenge: Take some time to think about an area of your life you're struggling with, then flip the script and remember the first time.

Positive Affirmation of the Day: I love _____! Fill in the blank with something or someone you're struggling with, and allow yourself to start loving again! (Do this in the mirror.)

Quote of the Day: "But there's always a first time for everything." —Melissa de la Cruz

DAY SIXTY-FOUR

Pay It Forward

CONGRATULATIONS ON MAKING it this far in our positive mindset journey! You've officially made it past two months and have less than thirty days left in your mindset transformation! You've likely already seen some significant changes in how you think and respond to situations in your life by using some of the information we've learned so far. So what's the next step? It's simple. *PAY IT FORWARD!!!*

A good friend of mine had a superior in the Marine Corps that taught him a valuable principle! He taught him: first you *"LEARN IT,"* then you *"DO IT,"* and finally you *"TEACH IT."* I love *"the learn it, do it, teach it"* philosophy, and I wish more people would use it. Ordinary people are willing to take the time to learn new things, apply them, and begin doing them to benefit themselves. What the extraordinary people in the world are doing, though, is that third step. They are then teaching it! What happens when you teach it is incredible! *YOU MASTER IT!*

Can you imagine being able to master all of the ideas and concepts in the pages of this book? From positive affirmations to becoming what we think about, gratitude and the gratitude journal, PMA, faith, desire, overcoming fear, giving, goals, thinking big, exercise and healthy eating, balance in life, love, and many other success principles! Do you think your life would change if you even mastered a few of these success skills? Your life would improve exponentially by just learning and doing these things. Imagine what your life could become if you'd share these principles with others and help them understand the things you've learned. You'd become a *MASTER* of positive thinking and have the most positive mindset you could ever imagine. I want that. Do you?

Now for the best news, it's 100% possible for you to do just that. All you have to do from today on is pay it forward. From today forward after reading each day, make it a point to share what you learned with coworkers, friends, and family members! The fringe benefit is that the people around you may join you in the journey for a more positive mindset. We become just like the people we hang around the most, so it will be imperative for you to share this with the people in your life. What are you waiting for? SHARE AWAY! Let's get you to that *MASTER* status!!!

Today's Challenge: Pick your favorite topic we've shared in the book thus far and share that with someone you love today! If they are receptive, challenge them to read this book too.

Positive Affirmation of the Day: I will learn it, do it, then teach it! (Do this in the mirror.)

Quote of the Day: "When you learn, teach. When you get, give." —Maya Angelou

DAY SIXTY-FIVE

Make Today Great

EVERY MORNING WHEN we wake up, we have a choice to make. It's simple: *MAKE TODAY GREAT!* Choose it every single day! Is it easy at first? Nope! Is it possible once you develop the habit? Absolutely! It's about starting your day with positive morning habits. I'll share some good ones with you to help you get started living a happier life now! Are you AWAKE? Then decide to make today great!

GRATITUDE: Every day I wake up and immediately thank God for another day. Being grateful gets the day started on a positive note. I pray for a minute or two before getting out of bed. This prayer isn't about asking God for things I want or need; it's about gratitude and thanking God for everything I already have! It takes one–two minutes and helps you realize what you already have to be thankful for.

HEALTHY: Making every meal healthy is difficult, but I've found breakfast the easiest. We can't expect to get good things out of our bodies and minds if we aren't putting good into them. So start your day with a healthy meal; this is good for the body and your mind, spirit, and mood. If you have time to exercise, do that too. I exercise in the afternoon/early evening, but I know many successful people who do it in the morning to help start the day right! Exercise is a mood changer.

POSITIVE AFFIRMATIONS: Doing positive affirmations in the morning dramatically impacts our mood for the rest of the day. All we are trying to do is set a great mood for the day early on, as we all know each day will bring challenges, and the attitude we set earlier in the day will determine how we deal with those challenges. Since you've made it this far in the book, I assume you already know how to do positive affirmations. Do them in the morning, every morning!

So there you have it! Morning habits that will change your life if you adopt them. If you don't have much extra time in your morning, exercise later in the day, that's what I do. However prayer/gratitude only takes one–two minutes; you could even do it while brushing your teeth or showering *(multitasking)*. You'll eat anyway, so grab a piece of fruit instead of Pop-Tarts, and you can do positive affirmations in the car on your way to work.

Today's Challenge: Do these three things starting tomorrow for a month and watch what happens to your morning mood.

Positive Affirmation of the Day: I have good morning habits that make me happy! (Do this in the mirror.)

Quote of the Day: "You don't have to be great to start, but you have to start to be great." —Zig Ziglar

Take a Break

SOMETIMES WHEN WE go too hard toward attaining our goals, we can end up in a phase of life I call *burnout!* It's essential to allow ourselves to *TAKE A BREAK* when we start to feel overwhelmed with life and all it brings. Stress is inevitable, and when it comes, it's vital to know when it's time to sit back for a day or two and re-adjust mentally before we jump back into the game of life.

Depending on your situation, you can get the recharge you need by taking a day; sometimes it'll take two. Other times it may require an actual getaway like a vacation with the family or a fishing/camping trip with no cell phone where you can unplug from the world. A trip to somewhere fun that will take your mind off of the grind of life that has you feeling burnt out! So today's message is simple: when you start to feel overwhelmed, *TAKE A BREAK!*

Below is a list of signs you're heading for burnout:

- Feeling bored with things that usually excite you
- Losing interest in your goals
- Work feels like WORK
- Not sleeping well (too much on your mind)
- Bad eating habits
- Drinking alcohol to cope
- Irritability
- Getting sick easier
- Anger
- Mental exhaustion

Everyone will experience different signs when we are heading toward burnout. We must know our signs to recognize them and do something to get ourselves out of the funk before it's too late and we reach the burnout phase. If you feel like you're in the burnout phase now…that's ok. I've been there myself more often than I'd like to admit; recognize it, then take a break and return to a positive mindset.

It's necessary to *SLOW DOWN* in life from time to time! After all life is supposed to be fun and exciting. When we go too hard and forget to rest and relax, life can become a grind, and that's no fun. Know the signs, and catch yourself when you're drifting down the path of potential burnout, then take a step back and take the break you need. You'll thank yourself later.

Today's Challenge: Evaluate your current situation in life to be sure you don't have any signs listed above that indicate burnout could be coming, then respond accordingly.

Positive Affirmation of the Day: My life is fun and exciting! (Do this in the mirror.)

Quote of the Day: "Sometimes the best solution is to rest, relax, and recharge. It's hard to be your best on empty." —Sam Glenn

Day Sixty-Seven

Get Back at It

NOW THAT WE took that break yesterday, we must get back at it right away! There is never a better time to go after your goals and dreams than immediately after you take a break and escape it all for a while. Whether you took one or two days to rest and recharge your battery or needed a little more time, I hope you are ready to get back to chasing whatever it is in your life you want to be, do, and have.

Take some time today to review your current goals and assess your progress. If you're on track and feel good about what you find, that's awesome; if not that's ok too! Just know that it's vital after stepping back and taking a break that we reassess to be sure we are on track and that they are still goals we desire to achieve. After all there is always a reason we start to feel burnt out...one of those reasons can be that our goals are no longer fulfilling to us. In this case we should look at and rethink some of them. If we aren't waking up early and staying up late thinking about our dreams, it's time to consider setting new goals to get us excited again!

Life is about a lot of things, and one of the most important things is staying hungry and excited every day. If you aren't waking up fired up and ready to take on the world, it's time to look at your goals or lack thereof and rewrite the life you want to have. Return to *(days twenty-eight and twenty-nine)* and repeat the process. It's worth it to take the time to redo your goals if you aren't motivated to chase them anymore. One of the worst traps to get caught up in is having goals that don't excite you anymore; that's a recipe for boredom and mediocrity.

None of you picked up this book because you enjoyed being bored and wanted to be average. You're reading this book because you're one of the special people who wants to be somebody. What are you waiting for? Reassess your goals *TODAY*, not tomorrow! Then if needed set some new big audacious goals that will keep you up late at night and wake you up early each morning because you're too excited to sleep!

Today's Challenge: Reassess your goals *TODAY!* If they don't excite you, get to work rewriting them!

Positive Affirmation of the Day: My goals give my life meaning! I am motivated! (Do this in the mirror.)

Quote of the Day: "Our greatest glory is not in never falling, but in rising every time we fall." —Confucius

DAY SIXTY-EIGHT

The Obstacles of Life

HAVE YOU EVER had something bad happen unexpectedly? An obstacle? If you answered yes, congratulations, you're normal. Life's obstacles come in all different sizes; some are huge and seem impossible, like losing a family member or a close friend. Others are much smaller and a part of our daily lives. All of them disrupt our lives.

Obstacles are a part of life whether we like it or not, and they usually come at the wrong time. Let me ask you a question. When is a good time to have something bad happen? *NEVER! S*ince we know that bad things happen even to good people, it's important to make sure we are mentally prepared when they do. Today I'll offer four tips to overcome *the obstacles of life.*

The first thing I do when facing adversity is to *PRAY.* God is always right there, and it's therapeutic talking to God during tough times. Prayer works! Reach out and ask others to pray for you too. We all have those prayer warriors who are just waiting to help. Ask for their help!

Next *THINK* about what you're dealing with, and if possible *DEVELOP A PLAN* to get yourself through it. Thinking about it and planning even works with matters of the heart, like losing a loved one; reflecting and thinking about all the good times you had with that person is therapeutic. So after you pray, get your thinking cap on. Keep praying through it all.

The third tip is to *REACH OUT FOR HELP!* Remember you'll never go through anything that someone you know hasn't already gone through. Reach out to someone you know that has had a similar experience to what you're going through and get their advice. Listen, and use their personal experience to get you through.

Lastly *TAKE ACTION.* After you've taken the time to pray, you spent some time thinking and developing a plan and reached out to others who had had a similar experience. Now it's time to take the most challenging step: take whatever action you find necessary to get you through the adversity. Will it be easy? *NOPE!* Will it be worth it? *YES!*

Always remember that anything and everything *is* possible to overcome! We will all have obstacles in our lives; what we do when they come will determine whether they are a simple hurdle or a brick wall that devastates our lives. Follow the tips in today's message; they've worked repeatedly for me.

Today's Challenge: Think back to your last big obstacle and then think about how applying those four tips would've helped you overcome it.

Positive Affirmation of the Day: I'm an overcomer, strong, and able! (Do this in the mirror.)

Quote of the Day: "The friend in my adversity I shall always cherish most. I can better trust those who helped to relieve the gloom of my dark hours than those who are so ready to enjoy with me the sunshine of my prosperity." —Ulysses S Grant

Day Sixty-Nine

A Fresh Start

LET'S FACE IT we all have times when we look at where we are and realize it isn't where we want to be. A positive mindset and a *FRESH START* mentality are essential in these moments! Nothing is wrong with not being where you want to be in your life; the problem sets in if and when we get stuck there and give up on our hopes and dreams. Getting stuck happens to many of us simply because we let it get to our heads when we aren't growing as fast as we expected or going through a trial. In these moments we must step back to inspect *what we expect* to get out of our lives moving forward. Tomorrow (day seventy) I'll cover how to do just that. *Inspect what you expect*. But for today let's get back to the subject at hand.

When we think about our lives, most of us will realize that even though we may not feel like we are where we want to be, we are right where we dreamed of being five, ten, or even fifteen years ago. In other words we are making progress even when it doesn't feel like it. It's important to recognize this, and it helps to look back at how far we've come. So pat yourself on the back for getting where you are today.

With that said there are times when we do need a *fresh start*. Job loss, relationship issues, family problems, an illness, or losing a loved one are times when a *fresh start* with a new mentality may be in order. Times like these in our lives are why I wrote this book and why developing a positive mindset is so important. Life becomes much more manageable when we find a way to look for the positive in every situation. So if you need a *fresh start* right now, take a deep breath, look back at how far you've come, pat yourself on the back, and prepare yourself for the new and improved life you want and deserve. It begins with brainstorming what you want your life to look like one, five, or even ten years from now.

Next go back (days twenty-eight and twenty-nine) to help yourself set new goals for your *fresh start*. The most important step you'll ever take is the first one. So what are you waiting for? Get to it! Take action, rewrite your life how you want it to be, and get after it! I talk about goals a lot because they are vital to a successful life and the roadmap we all need to get where we want.

If you read today's message and feel good about where you are, that's fantastic. I'm happy that things are going well for you. Keep using the positive habits you've developed. But go ahead and bookmark this page just in case a storm of life comes at you unexpectedly. Storms of life are inevitable; the stronger our mindset, the easier it will be to have a *fresh start* mentality when the thunder starts rolling and the lightning strikes.

Today's Challenge: Go back to (days twenty-eight and twenty-nine) and review the process of setting goals; if you need a *fresh start,* go ahead and set new goals for the new life you want and deserve.

Positive Affirmation of the Day: My life is mine, and I will live my dreams! (Do this in the mirror.)

Quote of the Day: "Take the first step in faith. You don't have to see the whole staircase, just take the first step." —Martin Luther King Jr.

Day Seventy

You're an Overcomer

HAVE YOU EVER had one of those days where nothing seemed to go your way? How about an entire week, month, or even longer? Possibly you've even had a season of life where it seemed nothing could go your way. A lost job, a failed marriage, or worse you've lost a loved one. If any of the above apply to you, you're not alone. If there is one thing I know for sure in our lives, there will be tough times and challenges that feel insurmountable when they come. However with all the confidence in the world, I can tell you that no challenge or trial of life can keep you down forever. *YOU'RE AN OVERCOMER!*

The Bible tells us that *"God made us in his image"* (Genesis 1:27). That's all I need to know to understand that He created us to be strong enough to get through life's challenges. So what are you going through right now? Does it feel impossible and insurmountable? Believe me when I tell you, it's not! The Bible also says, *"I can do all things through Christ who strengthens me"* (Philippians 4:13). So my first suggestion to anyone going through a hard time is to lean into God and pray about it. Ask God for the wisdom, confidence, comfort, and strength to get through it. At the time of this writing, just two short months ago, I lost my older brother Jeremy completely unexpectedly on Thanksgiving Day. To say it's been challenging would be an understatement. However, once again, it tells us in the Bible, *"with man, this is impossible, but with God all things are possible"* (Matthew 19:26). Leaning into God during the hard times and tough days is how I've been able to cope. I'm not insinuating that problems or losses go away just by talking to God, but He will show us how to ease them. The Bible also says, *"And this too shall pass"* (2 Corinthians 4:17-18). *That's* a scripture to hold onto during the difficult times of life! God will show you…*YOU'RE AN OVERCOMER!*

The tough times of life are also when having a built-in positive mindset will take you a long way. Even after losing my brother, I've found strength and happiness in all of the moments and memories my brother and I and our family shared all the years we got with him. I can't imagine going through a time like this without a healthy mindset. Working on and developing a positive mindset is necessary; we never know when a tragedy may strike and must always be mentally prepared. My second suggestion today is to keep working on your mental health, reading books like this one, hanging around positive people, listening to uplifting and positive podcasts and music, YouTube videos, etc. Doing all those things has helped me through one of the worst events in my life these past couple of months. Has it been easy? No! But has it been more manageable due to my suggestions today? Yes! Life is hard. Take care of your mental health; you never know when you'll need the extra strength. And remember...*YOU'RE AN OVERCOMER!*

Dedication: Today is dedicated to my brother Jeremy Wolbers. I love and miss you!

Today's Challenge: Read the three Bible verses I quoted in today's message, then believe what those verses are telling you!

Positive Affirmation of the Day: I am an OVERCOMER! (Do this in the mirror.)

Quote of the Day: "Although the world is full of suffering, it is also full of the overcoming of it." —Helen Keller

Day Seventy-One

Winning Isn't Everything

Zig Ziglar used to say, "Money isn't everything…but it ranks right up there with oxygen." I always loved hearing him say that because it was funny yet true. I feel like winning can be put in those exact terms; while winning isn't everything, it ranks pretty high for most of us if we are honest. I mean who likes losing?

The problem with winning is that, in some cases, there can only be one *"actual winner."* This is true in sporting events, most sales organizations, games, elections, and numerous other areas of our lives. Does this mean that everyone else who competed or *"lost"* is a loser? No way! The person or team that loses is often the biggest winner! How is that, you ask? Well, I don't know about you, but I've learned much more from my "losses" than my wins.

Don't get me wrong; I'm not suggesting that we should set out in any area of our lives to lose; instead that we should look at our losses afterward, readjust, learn, get back out there, and do it better the next time. Does this type of mentality guarantee a victory the next time? Nope! It guarantees that we will constantly improve; it also ensures a winning attitude and mindset that will lead to future wins. Your attitude and mindset make you a winner, not a trophy or award. However with this mindset, your trophy case won't sit empty for long.

When I was in high school, we had one of the top cross-country programs in Iowa. Several state champion runners came through our program (Dubuque Senior). In my senior year, a freshman came in with all the natural running ability anyone could imagine, and he went on to win two state championships in a row. But his senior year, one of his teammates kept learning and training hard, and while he didn't have the same God-given ability to run, he beat the two-time state champion their senior year and won a state title himself. The moral of the story: just because he didn't *"win"* the previous years didn't make him a *"loser"*; he was learning and growing. His victory came after several losses. You see failures don't make you a loser; you only lose when you give up!

I've seen it repeatedly in my own business experience where people who *"win"* get arrogant and then get passed up in the end by the very people they were beating. Why does this happen? When people lose and get determined to learn from it, they become highly motivated to win the next time. In many cases when they become successful, the very thing they credit most to their success is those previous losses! So you can see why I say **winning isn't everything;** it's more about what we do after the losses in life that will determine our future.

Today's Challenge: Think of a time when today's message pertained to you. What did you do after you lost? Did you quit or get determined to win the next time? Challenge yourself to dust yourself off, learn, readjust, and win the next time.

Positive Affirmation of the Day: I keep going no matter what. (Do this in the mirror.)

Quote of the Day: "Strength does not come from winning. Your struggles develop your strengths. When you go through hardships and decide not to surrender, that is strength." —Arnold Schwarzenegger

DAY SEVENTY-TWO

Stay Humble

WE ALL KNOW people who seem stuck on themselves. The kind of person who doesn't need anyone to pat them on the back for their achievements as they are good at doing it for themselves. How does that kind of person make you feel when you're around them? Small, not enough, inferior, etc.? That personality type is one you may want to steer clear of. Listening to that type of banter regularly isn't good for our mindset. It's hard to avoid in certain relationships as it may be a sibling, parent, or coworker you can't get away from. Most of us do it occasionally and don't realize it. My advice today is simple. No matter what is going on in your life, good or bad, *STAY HUMBLE!*

It can be challenging after big wins and achievements not to want to tell the world about what we just did or accomplished. It's ok to tell your inner circle about the highlights in your life. The problem comes in when we take it too far and become braggadocios. No one likes to listen to someone who seems self-absorbed! Successful people don't have to tell other people they are successful; people can tell by the way they act and carry themselves. Being humble and successful is attractive to others; you'll gain much respect for remaining humble through your success journey.

Here are a few good examples of people who stayed humble through wildly successful lives. Michael Jordan didn't have to tell anyone about his success on the basketball court; his performance showed them; he was humble. Oprah Winfrey didn't have to tell anyone how good she was; her actions showed it; she was humble. You never hear Warren Buffet, one of the wealthiest people in the world, talking about how much money he has. Other people do that for him; he is humble. If people can have that level of success and not brag about themselves, we can too. *Stay humble!*

There isn't a single person on the planet who hasn't bragged about themselves a little at some point, so don't beat yourself up if you've done it. Just catch and humble yourself before the world does it for you, and the world will do it for you!

Today's Challenge: Think about a time in your life when someone who wasn't humble made you feel inferior, then vow never to be that person to someone else.

Positive Affirmation of the Day: I am humble. I say and do things that build others up! (Do this in the mirror.)

Quote of the Day: "You're either humble or you're not. If you were a jerk before the fame, you just become a jerk with a bigger spotlight. Whoever you are really comes through." —Oprah Winfrey

DAY SEVENTY-THREE

Get Excited

I HAVE BEEN in the same business for almost thirty years at the time of this writing. While my role has changed over the past three decades, one thing has remained the same. I'm constantly selling. Whether it be selling myself, ideas, people, programs, or actual products, I've had to learn the art of persuasion, and let me tell you, it's easier than you might think. I'm in a sales business, so it's my job to sell every day. Without question one of the most important things to remember when trying to persuade anyone of anything is to be excited. Excitement sells! *GET EXCITED!*

When people find out what I do for a living, many of them tell me, "There is no way I could ever sell anything to anyone." While in reality we all sell every day. Whether you're doing something as simple as trying to sell your spouse or significant other on where to go for breakfast, lunch, or dinner, or maybe a more important issue like trying to convince your child to study before watching TV or getting on one of their devices, we are all selling our way through every day. The question is are you getting anyone to buy what it is you're trying to sell? Whether or not "salesperson" is your job title, you must learn the art of persuasion. Do you want to get your way in life? *GET EXCITED!*

I'm not suggesting you be manipulative; instead learn to be more persuasive by getting excited about your thoughts and ideas. The difference between a good salesperson and a con man is simple. Good salespeople have conviction about what they are selling and believe it's a win for themselves and the person they are trying to persuade. A con, on the other hand, is simply trying to get their way, whether it helps the other party or not. So as long as you have conviction and honestly believe it's for the best for both parties, *GET EXCITED* and start living the life you want.

How does this make any difference in whether or not I can develop and maintain a positive mindset? My response is simple: getting your way isn't always the most important thing, but it's nice to get it sometimes. Today's topic has everything to do with transforming your mind and life. It will lead to a defeated mindset if you're constantly going through life never getting what you want and getting run over by anyone and everyone. So today I'm trying to help you to avoid going through your life and never getting what you want by teaching you the most basic sales principle. *GET EXCITED,* and people will follow...

As you go through each day, you will experience many situations where you will either sell someone on your idea or they will convince you of theirs. Either way someone ends up getting sold. Do you want to go through life settling for everyone else's ideas, or would you like to be the one doing the convincing? *GET EXCITED!*

Today's Challenge: Be excited about everything you want to do today, then watch as other people gather to do it with you.

Positive Affirmation of the Day: My opinion matters, and I will sell it more often. (Do this in the mirror.)

Quote of the Day: "I have always said that everyone is in sales. Maybe you don't hold the title of salesperson, but if the business you are in requires you to deal with people, you, my friend, are in sales." —Zig Ziglar

DAY SEVENTY-FOUR

Happiness Is a Choice

EVERY MORNING WE wake up and face a critical decision. This choice will ultimately set the tone for how the day will go. We have two options.

First we can buy into the fact that we didn't get enough sleep, are still tired, and, maybe for some of us, are even a little grumpy. We can bring yesterday's troubles to the forefront of our minds, think about the stresses of life, and make a conscious decision to start our day on the wrong foot. This choice usually leads to a bad day, and we've all been there. When we make this choice, we are choosing to be unhappy!

Or we can take what we've learned in the previous seventy-three days and decide to wake up and say, yes, I'm a little tired, but if I get out of bed, listen to some uplifting music, grab a cup of coffee, text someone and tell them I love them, read something positive, pray and ask God for a great day, have a healthy breakfast, maybe even get a quick workout in, do some positive affirmations, look at our goals, be thankful for everything that we already have, and thank God for waking us up for yet another day, this one is also a conscious decision, but it's the decision that will lead to us being happy today and usually leads to a great day!

I'm saying that **happiness is a choice** we all get to make every day, and it's the only choice that leads to us developing and eventually maintaining a positive mindset. We have to make waking up and choosing to be happy a habit.

James Clear, an author and habit expert, wrote a book titled *Atomic Habits*. In the book he talks about how long it takes to develop a habit, and he says it was a common thought that it took twenty-one days. After further study it takes just over two months to truly make something a habit (sixty-six days to be exact).

149

So give it some time and be patient with yourself. But, by all means, start consciously thinking happy thoughts in the morning when you first wake up and do at least some of the things listed above to develop good morning habits that will determine how the rest of your day will go. Do you want to have a good day? Choose happiness in the morning! Do you want to be happy? Choose your thoughts and habits carefully; it's up to you! Happiness is a choice!

Today's Challenge: Consciously think happy thoughts when you wake up tomorrow morning; if you need to, write yourself a note by your bedside as a reminder. Then do it again the next day. (Post-it notes on the bathroom mirror work great for this.)

Positive Affirmation of the Day: I am a happy person. I choose to be happy every day. (Do this in the mirror.)

Quote of the Day: "Happiness depends upon ourselves." —Aristotle

Day Seventy-Five

Vision

Anyone who opens this book and reads at least one page has some idea of what they want their life to be like. So why is it that only some of us will use the material and see our lives change as a result of it? The answer is that only some of us will have the clear vision necessary to follow through and live the life we desire. The fact that you have made it to day seventy-five tells me that you are indeed one of those special people who not only say you want to live a certain way, but are willing to put in the time and effort to make it happen! You, my friend, have a true *VISION!*

One good way to help us take our goals and dreams and make them a reality is to create a dream/vision board. If you've never heard of such a thing, you're in for a life-changing lesson today.

A dream/vision board is where you take a poster board, cut out all kinds of pictures and phrases that match your goals and dreams and glue/tape them to the board for you to look at every day. There's just something about seeing something you want every day, it makes it real in your mind, and you start believing it could happen. It gives you a vision of your goals and dreams, and we all know the old saying, *"Seeing is believing."*

For many years Tara and I wanted to build our "dream home." So what did we do? If you said to print out pictures of the home of our dreams and put them on a dream/vision board, you would be correct. When we put it on our dream/vision board, we had no idea how to make that goal a reality; we just believed we would. Seeing it every day motivated us to do the work necessary to make our goals and dreams a reality. I'm happy to announce that in 2020, we made that dream a reality and built the home of our dreams. Putting that home on a dream/vision board made it a reality to us before it happened. We've got countless other goals that have come to fruition in large part due to the belief that putting them on a dream/vision board brought to us. We are living proof in many areas that these work.

I understand that doing some of the things I've recommended in this book may seem a little odd to you at first, but these crazy ideas work, and by the way, they seemed weird to me at first too. But I wanted to live my dreams and was willing to give anything at least one shot! I am glad I tried the dream/vision board; it changed my life by helping me get a literal vision of my goals and dreams. So what are you waiting for? Catch a *VISION* today and make your dreams a reality!

Today's Challenge: Research dream/vision boards, try Google or YouTube, then make one of your own and watch your dreams start to come true.

Positive Affirmation of the Day: I have a true vision of what I want my life to look like. I'm willing to do whatever it takes to live my dreams. (Do this in the mirror.)

Quote of the Day: "The only thing worse than being blind is having sight but no vision." —Helen Keller

DAY SEVENTY-SIX

Live Your Dreams

WE ALL HAVE those big dreams we wish to do, be, or have. Whether it's a job we'd be excited to have, a vacation we've always wanted to go on, or maybe yours is to get married and live happily ever after with the love of your life. There is no limit to the dreams we have in our hearts and minds. Today I want to help you realize that every single one of those dreams is still possible for you and that you can *live your dreams!*

What are those dreams for you? Go ahead, take a minute right now, and think about it. Next please take a minute to think about this next question. What is holding you back from chasing and eventually living those dreams?

The reason, as adults, we start losing the enthusiasm to chase after our dreams is *what-if thinking.* We all have *"what if"* thinking sometimes, and we need to change our thoughts after the words *"what if."*

So instead of saying or thinking, *"What if"* I don't have enough time or money? *"What if"* I lack the confidence and self-esteem to achieve my dreams? *"What if"* I'm in bad health? *"What if"* my job gets in the way or my spouse or family isn't supportive?

We should instead say and think, *"What if"* I had all the extra time I needed? *"What if"* money wasn't an object? *"What if"* I could work on my self-confidence and have healthy self-esteem? *"What if"* my health was perfect and my job allowed me the time and resources I want and need to live my desired life? *"What if"* I have the support of a loving spouse and family?

When we change the words we say and think after those *"What ifs"* in our minds, we take power back and will start to see the positive changes in our lives and truly begin to take the actions necessary to live our dreams, and fear and doubt will no longer hold us back.

You weren't put here on this earth to be average or less than others! You're here to shine bright and to wake up every day believing in the power of your dreams! Remember when you were a child and you thought you could do, be, and or have anything in life you wanted? Do you know why most kids feel that way? You'd be right if you guessed because they don't worry or doubt how it will happen! Too often, as adults, we overanalyze how we could do, be, or have something that seems so big, and then, in the end, we stop trying to attain it. That's the absolute worst thing we can do! Get out there and live your dreams!

Today's Challenge: Answer the two questions in the second paragraph. What are your dreams? What's holding you back? Then work on your thoughts and words that follow the *"what ifs."*

Positive Affirmation of the Day: I deserve to live my dreams! (Do this in the mirror.)

Quote of the Day: "Don't give up on your dreams, or your dreams will give up on you." —John Wooden

Momentum

As WE NEAR the end of our ninety-day transformation, I hope that your mindset, life, and the lives of those you love have changed. I'd be surprised if you have not seen any significant changes in your thoughts. *(Remember we do become what we think about. See day three.)* Reading a book like this is an excellent step toward developing the positive mindset we all want and deserve. What's important now is to continue with the new and improved daily habits we've learned and maintain the positive changes we've made these past few months! You've come this far, and you now have ***momentum!*** Let's keep it going!

Lou Holtz, former coach of the Notre Dame Fighting Irish football team, had a mantra that he used when coaching his players. He taught them the acronym WIN *(What's Important Now?)*. He wanted his players to be laser-focused on today and not worry about what happened yesterday or what will happen tomorrow. This type of mindset is perfect for us to learn and adopt at this stage of our mindset journey. What's important now for all of us is to continue to use the ideas and concepts we've learned thus far in our daily lives. If you've been doing the things suggested in the previous seventy-six days, then you've already developed many new positive daily habits. Congratulations! Now if you keep them going, there is no doubt your mindset and life will be changed forever. It's called momentum, and chances are good you have it right now.

Motivational speaker Zig Ziglar used to say all the time. *"People often say that motivation doesn't last. Well, neither does bathing; that's why we recommend it daily."* While this quote would always get a good laugh from his live audiences, it was and still is very accurate. Much like motivation when we get some positive momentum in our lives, we must continue the daily habits that got us there. The good thing about momentum is that it's easy to keep going if we continue to do what got us there. The bad thing is that it's just as easy to lose if we get lazy and revert to our old habits. I trust that since you're still with me and reading on day seventy-seven, you will keep the momentum going and continue to live the life you desire and deserve to live. If you feel yourself slipping into your old habits, ask yourself one question: What's important now? Then do that and get your momentum back!

Today's Challenge: Answer this question: What's important now? Then do that!

Positive Affirmation of the Day: I have a positive mindset and will do whatever it takes to keep it! (Do this in the mirror.)

Quote of the Day: "Momentum solves 80% of your problems." —John C. Maxwell

You're an Original

When you look in the mirror, what do you see? Who do you see? Does the reflection show you a person that God put here on purpose, for a purpose? That's who and what you are. **You're an original** made by God on purpose and for a purpose.

We've reached the point in this book and mindset challenge where we understand that it's our choice to wake up every day believing we are here for a reason. We've all heard the expression, *"Everything happens for a reason."* I'm here to tell you that EVERYONE happens for a reason too! You matter, your life matters, you have greatness inside you, you can inspire others, and God loves you and made you for a reason. The world needs you and what you have to offer.

You may wonder what could I possibly contribute to this world? We develop the misconception that we have to be wealthy, a person of influence, or even famous to make an impact in the lives of others. That couldn't be further from the truth. In 2015 when we lost our nephew to cancer, Tara decided that she would make a difference for people who were sick and suffering. She has no formal background in the medical field, but what she does have is a little extra time and a good heart for volunteering. That's just what she did, and she now volunteers once per week at our local hospital, helping in any way she can. She's making a difference in the lives of others. Why? Because she decided that even though she didn't have an education in medicine, she could still make a difference for people fighting illness. You, too, can make a difference in this world by doing something in an area you're passionate about.

What does volunteering at a hospital have to do with being an original? It has everything to do with it; we all have different God-given gifts and talents that make us original. No one else in the world has the exact DNA you do, so that makes each of us unique. What we do with our originality is up to us. Tara chooses to help others with her time by volunteering. I am more of a giver of knowledge and resources. I find my purpose by inspiring others to live their best lives and giving from the resources God has blessed me with. We are all different and original; what's important is finding what inspires us and then using it for other people's good. We all have something that someone else needs. What makes you original?

Today's Challenge: Take time to brainstorm and write down ten things that excite you about life. Narrow those down to two or three things that inspire you. You've just found a few things that make you original.

Positive Affirmation of the Day: I'm unique. I can make a difference in the lives of others. (Do this in the mirror.)

Quote of the Day: "You were born an original, don't die a copy." —John Mason

DAY SEVENTY-NINE

Spread Love

THERE'S JUST SOMETHING special about spending time with the right kind of people. I'm talking about those who understand and live by the "Golden Rule" (*see day six*). The people that bring the mood up a notch when they walk into a room. Uplifting people who always seem to be smiling, saying nice things, or saying nothing at all. You know the type, right? The people who always ***spread love*** and make everyone around them feel special. Most people with these qualities don't even realize it, but everyone around them does! Who knows? You may even be that person yourself!

The Golden Rule means *treating others as you would like to be treated;* some people are just really good at living that out. Today I want to take a closer look at the qualities of "Golden Rule" people and examine what we can do to be that person ourselves. Who doesn't want to be known as that kind of person?

Golden Rule Qualities

- Joy filled
- Smile and laugh often
- Optimistic about their life
- Talk positively about others; you'll rarely hear them speak badly of anyone
- Good listeners
- Polite
- They believe in the law of reciprocity (what goes around comes around)

I have some good news for you. All the qualities listed above are habits we can all learn and adopt. If you look at the list, it's simple decisions that we can all be making every day. That's what people who live by the Golden Rule do; they choose to be friendly, full of joy, smile when others are around, talk positively about themselves and others, listen when spoken to, and be polite! The law of reciprocity is just a byproduct of the decisions they make. In other words other people treat them great because that's how they treat them. It's kind of like magic. Do you want to be loved? Spread love yourself first, and love will bounce right back your way like a boomerang!

Today's Challenge: Consciously work on two of the Golden Rule qualities listed above today and watch as others will follow your lead and treat you better.

Positive Affirmation of the Day: I live by the Golden Rule! (Do this in the mirror.)

Quote of the Day: "Do unto others as you would have them do unto you." —Jesus

Decide

ACCORDING TO VARIOUS internet sources, on average we are faced with 35,000 choices per day (google it); researchers at Cornell University found that 227 of those choices are on just food alone. Making decisions is just a part of our daily routine, and we make most of them without a second thought, like what to wear or what to eat for breakfast or lunch. Then we make more meaningful choices, like where to live, what to do for a living, where to send our kids to school, and who we hang around and how often. You get the point; our lives are one decision after another, and our choices shape who we are and how we live. So our lives are what we decide them to be. See what I did there? Do you want a better life full of new and exciting opportunities? *DECIDE!*

Taking all of the above into account, I want to challenge you today to understand that our lives are a simple reflection of the decisions we make and/or have made in the past. That is good news for some and bad for others. Look we've all made bad decisions that have at least temporarily hurt us, and most of us will make more poor choices. I'm not suggesting that we beat ourselves up for past choices; quite the contrary. I recommend consciously thinking about the decisions we make moving forward. Past decisions are over with; we can't change those, good or bad. Would it interest you if I told you that you could change your life for the better in the next year simply by making more conscious decisions? Well, guess what? You can!

Make an overall decision to be more mindful of the small things, as those are the choices that lead to the big stuff. A good example would be making a small choice each day to eat a little healthier and work out five days a week for at least thirty minutes. Would that make a difference in the way you look and feel one year from now? Of course it would; you would benefit from that small healthy choice every day you looked in the mirror. Or what if you made a small choice to start doing positive affirmations and writing down five things you're grateful for every morning when you first wake up? That's a decision and choice that would make you a completely different person one year from now, which I hope you are after reading this book.

Today let's decide to steer your life in the direction you want it to go by making small choices that will lead to significant life changes. It all starts with one… one thought, one choice, one decision that could change not only your life, but your entire family tree. When you change people notice, and then they change too!

Today's Challenge: Make one healthy decision that you usually wouldn't. Eat a healthy breakfast, set new goals, or compliment someone. Start shaping your new and improved life today.

Positive Affirmation of the Day: I make good decisions that improve my life. (Do this in the mirror.)

Quote of the Day: "Sometimes you make the right decision, sometimes you make the decision right." —Dr. Phil McGraw

Faith over Fear

Whenever we have one of those big decisions, as discussed in yesterday's message, we will decide based on one of two powerful emotions: *faith or fear!* I hope that today's message persuades you to choose **faith over fear!**

Let's start with fear. Fear, by definition, means *an unpleasant emotion caused by the belief that someone or something is dangerous, likely to cause pain or a threat.* That's certainly not the attitude I want to go into a major life decision with. Don't get me wrong, I do want to weigh the good with the bad anytime I've got a decision to make that could change my life and the lives of those that I love, but to use a fear-based thought process in the decision would leave me with only one answer. What would that answer be? I'd be afraid to make any choices and would likely live without any changes. We all know that while change can be scary and causes some fear, it's inevitable for growth. So while I understand that you may fear making certain decisions, I'm asking you not to make decisions based on fear alone. It's making decisions based on fear that should scare us! Choose faith over fear.

Next let's discuss what making our decisions with faith as our guide would look like. Faith, by definition, means *complete trust or confidence in someone or something.* If you're thinking, "That's a crazy way to make decisions too!" You'd be right if you're talking about "blind faith." I'm talking about using faith mixed with common sense and even a little devil's-advocate thinking to make the big decisions in our lives. In no way, shape, or form am I suggesting that making decisions based on faith will be easy; it's just that if we are going to have a positive mindset and want happier, joy-filled lives, we need to use a faith-over-fear mentality in every area of our lives including decision making.

So today choose faith over fear in all areas of life, especially when faced with a potentially life-changing decision. Ask yourself this the next time you make a life-altering choice. What's the worst thing that could happen if I say yes? Then ask what's the worst thing that can happen if I turn it down or say no? Analyzing how you answer those two simple questions will usually be all you'll need to decide. Choose faith!

Today's Challenge: Think about the last difficult decision you had to make. Did you base it on faith or fear? How did it end up?

Positive Affirmation of the Day: I have a faith-over-fear mentality! (Do this in the mirror.)

Quote of the Day: "Always remember this; don't believe everything you think. Instead, replace your worries with faith." —Jeanette Coron

DAY EIGHTY-TWO

You've Gotta See It

TODAY I'M GOING to share an old quote with you that I love and live by: *"You've got to see it before you see it...so you can see it."* While that sure is a mouth full of "see its," if you slow down, read that back a few times, and think about the meaning, you'll realize it's excellent advice. It's simply saying that if you visualize your goals and dreams, you're far more likely to see them come true! When you become a visionary, you begin to take advantage of the power of your mind. ***You've gotta see it!***

When you make it a habit to visualize your goals and dreams, you begin to think about them all the time, daydream about them, and see yourself in the position where you've already accomplished them. It's almost like you have the magical power to make your dreams come true. And they will start to come true.

One of my biggest passions in life is to help YOU live your dreams. That's why I wrote this book. Being in sales my entire life and understanding how important a positive mindset is, it's my passion to share all the life lessons I've learned to help change the world one person at a time. But I can tell you with 100% confidence that this book would've never happened if I didn't first visualize the outcome. I had the book's cover done and the title picked out and written down well before I even wrote the first page. Why? I wanted it to become a reality, so I started "seeing it" as done. I even wrote "over 1 million copies sold" on the cover. I want to see that come true too. We must visualize what we want exactly how we want it.

To use a simple example of how powerful vision is, consider commercials advertising food and drinks. After you see the food in the commercial looking all perfect and with steam coming off it or hear the fizz of a soft drink, what do you want that night for dinner? What do you want to drink? That's right, you want what you just saw, and in many cases, that's what we do for dinner and what we drink to wash it down. Advertising experts understand how important it is to get the consumer to visualize their product or service. Here is the best part, you can do the same thing with your goals and dreams. What do you want in your life? See it in your mind so you can see it in your life!

Today's Challenge: Think of one thing you've wanted to do, be, or have in your life but it seems unrealistic. Visualize it as if it's already happened.

Positive Affirmation of the Day: I believe in my goals and dreams. I believe they will happen! (Do this in the mirror.)

Quote of the Day: "In order to carry a positive action, we must develop here a positive vision." —Dalai Lama

Enlarge Your Vision

YESTERDAY'S MESSAGE RELATED to learning how to see things in our minds to make them more believable. Being a visionary helps us attain our goals that were once dreams that seemed out of reach. It's so important to see things in our minds first as if they have already happened; it just does something in our subconscious mind that makes the unbelievable believable. The old saying *"seeing is believing"* is so true, and visualizing your goals and dreams as if they already happened is a great way to trick our minds into believing that anything is possible. Today I want to take it one step further and help you to ***enlarge your vision!***

Now that we understand the "see it before you see it, so you can see it" philosophy, let us dig deeper and start thinking and believing for more and bigger things in our lives. What is one big audacious goal or dream that you have that seems out of reach? Maybe it's a new car, higher education, your dream home, or perhaps you want to try something new and exciting like skydiving, surfing, skiing, or some other sport or recreation you've never allowed your mind to visualize yourself being able to do.

It comes down to getting yourself to buy in that achieving what you truly want is possible. How do you do that? I'm glad you asked. *You start thinking bigger and visualizing it as if it has already happened!* It works; like I said yesterday, it's like magic.

If it works so well, and we know that visualizing what we want to happen before it happens is so effective, then why not enlarge our vision and start going after what we really want? There are no limits for those who believe. So many people have done so many things that others said were impossible.

Roger Bannister broke the four-minute mile, we put a man on the moon, the internet, the automobile, how about the cell phone and the fact that a computer used to be the size of a large room and now it fits in our back pocket. These are examples of things that could've never happened if someone didn't first see it and then believed it was possible! If seeing is believing, we all must get our imaginations going and start seeing what we want to live out.

Today's Challenge: Visualize something you want as if you already have it. See it, and make it something great big!

Positive Affirmation of the Day: I can be, do, or have anything I put my mind to. (Do this in the mirror.)

Quote of the Day: "Having a vision for your life allows you to live out of hope, rather than out of your fears." —Stedman Graham

It's a Great Day to Be Alive

EVERY SINGLE DAY comes with new and exciting opportunities. Unfortunately most days bring problems and challenges as well. Each day is going to go exactly how we think it will go. If we choose to think about and focus on the problems and challenges, that day will likely prove to be challenging. Instead if we stay focused on each day's opportunities, we will find it infinitely easier to deal with those inevitable problems and challenges, remain positive, and make that day great! When we look for and focus on the positive and the new opportunities each day brings, we can genuinely say ***it's a great day to be alive!***

Every day is great to be alive, considering the alternative is not to be. Today I will challenge you to start saying out loud as a positive affirmation *"It's a great day to be alive"* every morning when you awaken. The more you say it, the more you'll believe it. That's another lesson in and of itself; we believe what we tell ourselves. So why not tell yourself good things and think positively about your life? Try it; you won't regret it; we do become what we tell ourselves we are! Who are you becoming?

Whenever life's problems and challenges get you down, you have to be mentally prepared to fight back with your new and improved positive mindset. That's precisely what this book is all about: developing a mental armor against all negativity that arises. By learning and then applying the information given in the pages of this book, you are doing that; you're putting on a mental armor against negativity. It's amazing how it works when you train your mind to see the negative immediately, then put it exactly where it belongs: in the permanent trashcan of your mind. You're going to love your new mindset. It will help you realize that every single day is a great day to be alive! Isn't that an excellent thought? Believe it! Say it every day! You'll start believing! If I did it, *YOU*, yes, I said *YOU*, can do it too!

What are you waiting for? Have a great day; it's a great day to be alive.

Today's Challenge: Decide that today will be great no matter what tries to get in your way! Put on your mental armor and make today great!

Positive Affirmation of the Day: I'm excited about my life; it's a great day to be alive. (Do this in the mirror.)

Quote of the Day: "We don't have a great day, we make it a great day." —Frosty Westering

DAY EIGHTY-FIVE

Live Your Purpose

PURPOSE, HAVE YOU found yours? Are you living it out? Or are you still searching for it? Whether you've discovered your purpose and are already living it out or you're still digging down deep trying to find it, it's positive to stop and think about the above questions and figure out where you're at so you can set your goals accordingly, make a plan for moving forward, and take massive action toward living your best life. A life lived on purpose, with a purpose, is much more fulfilling. So today, let's **find and live your purpose!**

What is a purpose, and what does living a life of purpose mean? Purpose means *the reason for which something is done or created or for which something exists.* So, when you think about your purpose, ask yourself, Why am I here? What makes me happy? What am I good at? Those three questions will help you define what your purpose may be. The "verb" definition of purpose is *to have as one's intention or objective.* So again, ask yourself a question. What is my intention in my life? What is my objective? If you think those are deep questions, good! They are! Defining your purpose isn't supposed to be easy; it's the reason you exist, so it's already inside you. You have to find it. Another good thing to do is to ask some close friends and family members those questions about you and see what they say.

If you have yet to find your purpose in life, that's ok. Continue asking the above questions of yourself and those close to you. Keep looking until you find what makes you so passionate that you lay awake in bed thinking about it late at night and wake up the following day with it still on your mind. When that happens, you've found it!

If you already know your purpose, congratulations! Your main objective now should be ensuring your goals are in balance with that purpose. Then continue to set more goals as you achieve the ones you already have. Stay the course, and keep that purpose in mind every day, all the time. Lastly, develop positive, healthy daily habits that will help you gradually fulfill that purpose in your life!

I've said this before, and I'll repeat it: YOU, yes, I did say *YOU* were put here on this earth for a purpose. *YOU* have to believe that! You will become exactly what you think yourself to be. Start telling yourself that you are here for a reason and then actively search for that reason/purpose every single day. Make it your passion first to find your purpose; once you do, live it out. I found mine in helping other people find theirs and then showing them meaningful and practical ways to live it out. That's why I wrote this book! It was my purpose! What's yours? Find it and then live it!

Today's Challenge: Take a few minutes to ask yourself every question I posed in today's message.

Positive Affirmation of the Day: I will find and live out my purpose in life! (Do this in the mirror)

Quote of the Day: "The purpose of life is not to be happy. It is to be useful, to be honorable, to be compassionate, to have it make some difference that you have lived and lived well." —Ralph Waldo Emerson

Day Eighty-Six

Create Some Luck

I DON'T BELIEVE in luck, but I love the old saying, *"The harder I work, the luckier I get."* When we prepare ourselves for success by doing things that most people won't, we could appear lucky from the outside looking in, and that couldn't be any further from the truth. We prepared for success and expected to win, so we did! Today's message is about being prepared for success and helping you ***create some luck!***

Today I'll share three ways to prepare for success. Since you've read this far, you already know that I believe it starts with setting some goals. If you've never set goals, go back to (Days 28-29) and follow those steps. So, the first way to prepare to create luck in our lives is to set goals, develop a plan to achieve them, then take action.

Next, we need to *get a checkup from the neck up!* We need a winning attitude. One way to help in that area would be to take some of your goals and turn them into positive affirmations, and talk about them as if you've already achieved them. Attitude is everything in life. When we believe in ourselves and start saying *"I can"* instead of *"I can't,"* we can change our lives and the lives of everyone around us.

Lastly, be aware of who you are hanging around and who is influencing you. We begin to act just like the people we spend the most time with. So, spend your time with people who will encourage you to be the best you can be, supportive people who have your best interest at heart and want to see you succeed. Having a great support group in our lives is vital to our success. Be that person for them too! It's a two-way street.

We all know people we look at and think they sure are lucky. Just remember that luck isn't even real, and they worked hard to get themselves into a position where others think they are lucky. They created that luck, and the best news is you can too!

Today's Challenge: Research the importance of a positive attitude. Just Google it, and you'll be amazed at how vital experts believe it is.

Positive Affirmation of the Day: I can and will live the life of my dreams! (Do this in the mirror)

Quote of the Day: "I'm a great believer in luck, and I find the harder I work the more I have of it." —Thomas Jefferson

Day Eighty-Seven

Changing The Channel

YOU'VE MADE IT through 86 days of our mindset challenge; congratulations. Has your mindset improved by reading the messages, accepting the challenges, doing the daily positive affirmations, and reading the quotes on these pages? I hope your answer to that question was a GREAT BIG YES. From my experience, developing a new and improved positive mindset changed my life forever, and everything written in the pages of this book has already worked for me. I used to live a very stressful life filled with anxiety and depression. Why? It was simple: I had developed bad habits and was allowing myself to think negatively, and I had a worst-case-scenario mindset rather than a best-case scenario. All that changed when I decided to think positively no matter what was happening around me. I live a normal life filled with the same ups and downs as everyone else. The most significant difference between the old and new me is that I focused on the ups, not the downs. Try it; it works wonders.

As we near the end of our journey together, it's just the beginning of the new and improved life you will be living due to your commitment to developing a more positive mindset. I'm excited for you. The next step is to continue with the positive daily habits you've developed in the past few months.

I will share with you one of the simplest yet most important exercises I've ever learned. I call it ***changing the channel!*** I wrote about it in a previous message, but it's so important and changed my life so much that I'm covering it again today so that it will be one of the last thoughts I leave you with.

What would you do if a song came on the radio that you didn't like? How bout your TV? What if a show you weren't interested in came on? What would you do? That's right; the answer is easy. You'd *change the channel* and listen or watch something you liked. Good news for you, your mind and thoughts work the same way. Whenever any scary, harmful, ugly, unpleasant, or fearful thought comes to mind, *CHANGE THE CHANNEL*. You are in complete control of your thoughts, and whenever negativity enters your mind, immediately and consciously *change the channel to* something more positive. It's just as easy to have good thoughts as bad ones.

So, the next time any thought enters your mind that isn't helpful, *change the channel!* When you do this day after day, it will become a habit. It's possible I did it, and my life has changed forever. Try it! I dare you!

Today's Challenge: The next time you have a negative thought, immediately replace it with a positive one. It will probably happen soon, so be ready. Start catching yourself when you think negatively; it will eventually become second nature.

Positive Affirmation of the Day: I think positive thoughts. (Do this in the mirror)

Quote of the Day: "Your mind is a powerful thing. When you filter it with positive thoughts, your life will start to change." —Buddha

Day Eighty-Eight

Be Prepared

How badly do you want a better life? How badly do you want success? How badly would you like better mental health? Physical health? Better relationships? How badly do you want joy and happiness? The road to success in all of these areas can be challenging. You'll have days when it doesn't feel worth it, days when you don't have the energy to do some of the things recommended in these pages. That's ok; allow yourself to have those moments and those days. You'll have some setbacks as you continue toward a more positive mindset. That's why it's essential to develop positive habits and then do them daily. Yes, even on the days when you don't feel like it. So, if you want to have a positive mindset, be successful, and achieve your goals and dreams in life, and I know you do, you have to *be prepared!*

Spiritually, mentally, and physically prepared for the ride of your life. Like all good things, developing and maintaining a positive mindset takes planning, preparation, and then that four-letter word so many people run from. *WORK!* Yep, it takes work; it will be challenging. Even positive people have negative moments. The difference lies in the preparation and work that those of us who have developed a positive mindset have put in. Preparing, planning, and constant learning help us through the weak moments. The good news is that anyone can do it! Yes, even you!!!! So, get ready for the ride of your life and be prepared to succeed.

Your journey starts now, and it will be fun and rewarding. It's also going to be trying and downright brutal at other times. I've always believed that just like the seasons of nature, we have seasons of life. Winter, Spring, Summer, and Fall. Winter is a tough season when we don't seem to grow; having a positive mindset makes the winters of life shorter and more tolerable. Then comes Spring, where we are planting but not reaping yet; that can be a tough season as we don't see results yet. Hang in there because it will grow as long as we nurture what we've planted. Next, we have Summer, a fun season where we keep pouring in the sunshine and watering what we planted in the Spring; we stay optimistic, knowing our crop will eventually sprout and grow. Summer is a busy yet fun season, where we are hard at work, looking forward to and feeling optimistic about the final season. Fall, that's the harvest season when we will see the growth happening and the fruits of our labor come to fruition. The harvest is the season that makes all the hard work and tough times worth it. It's important to envision the harvest during every other season; it keeps us motivated to keep going. So, be sure to prepare for all four seasons; you really can't outsmart them. It's the positive mindset that will get you through to your harvest!

Today's Challenge: Ask yourself the questions in the first paragraph, How bad do you want it?

Positive Affirmation of the Day: I am prepared for my successful journey. I have everything I need to live the life of my dreams. (Do this in the mirror)

Quote of the Day: "By failing to prepare, you are preparing to fail." —Benjamin Franklin

DAY EIGHTY-NINE

Do it Now

PLEASE DON'T PUT off to tomorrow what you could get done today; it's rarely good to put something important off. It's such a feel-good moment to know that it would have been easier to wait or do it later, but we chose to do it now! Feelings and emotions are important to acknowledge when developing and maintaining a positive mindset and attitude. When we decide to put important things off, and it is a choice, we are setting ourselves up for negative feelings and emotions, which can, in turn, set us back on our attitude and mindset. If something is important, get up, get moving, and ***do it now!***

Procrastination, by definition, means *the action of delaying or postponing something.* It's defined as an action even though it means not taking action. Im not sure about you, but I find putting things off stressful, and it's usually the only thing I can think about until I do it anyway. So why not just do it now so we can forget it and move on? You may wonder what this has to do with having a positive mindset. My answer is that it has everything to do with our ability to remain positive. Being constantly late and putting essential tasks and decisions off affects our brains. It fills us with negative emotions like worry, stress, and anxiety; honestly, if a person becomes a chronic procrastinator, it can lead to bad things like depression.

How do we change from putting things off to doing them now? Almost always, a simple change in our daily habits will lead us to a new mindset when prioritizing our lives. And what procrastination is at its roots is a priorities issue. When we re-prioritize and develop new daily habits based on what we believe is important in our lives, the change takes care of itself. Like most topics we've discussed, this one will be a challenging change, but it is necessary to maintain our sanity.

I want you to think about someone you know who is always late for everything; ask yourself, why are they always late? If your answer was mindset, then you got it right. People who are habitually late do so because they believe they will be late for everything; they've taught themselves to be late. The same is true with putting off what we can do today until tomorrow. It's a mindset that people teach themselves over time; then, they develop unhealthy habits that lead them always to put things off. They get used to saying no to doing it now and don't even realize the stress it's causing in their lives until it starts to spiral out of control, and it will spiral out of control. Procrastination leads to loss every time. Loss of jobs, relationships, and trust, to name just a few. So, today choose to start acting now on anything that you believe could cause stress by putting it off. You'll thank yourself later!

Today's Challenge: I want you to take care of the next important thing that comes up today right away, no waiting. Then, see how that makes you feel.

Positive Affirmation of the Day: I am a do-it-now person. I take action immediately when important things come up in my life. (Do this in the mirror)

Quote of the Day: "Do it now, sometimes later becomes never." —Unknown

What are you waiting for?

OVER THE PAST 90 days, we've covered everything from resetting and recharging our lives to setting new goals, doing positive affirmations, having a balanced life, living a healthy physical and mental lifestyle, and much more. So, the only thing left to do is to get out there and start living it! The life you've always dreamed of, the life you've always wanted for yourself but always thought it was only for other people, special people, privileged people. Well, I've got great news for you, you are that other person, you are special, you are privileged, and I'm asking you to believe that with me. You are a changed person now, fully equipped with a new mindset. A positive mindset you've always deserved to have.

The best time to act on new information is NOW! Tony Robbins says that we must first set a goal, then visualize the desired outcome, and finally TAKE MASSIVE ACTION…you see, too often in life, we are willing to take baby steps of setting a few new goals and even taking it to the next step and visualizing the desired outcome. But where does the rubber meet the road? If you said by getting after it, developing a plan, and then taking MASSIVE ACTION, you'd be correct! A goal without a plan and action is simply a thought on paper of something we may want someday. When we put a plan together and then take MASSIVE ACTION, our lives change and become what we want them to be.

What do you want your life to look like one year from now? How bout five years from now? Ten years? Etc. Guess what? It's your life, and you're the author of it. So, get to writing it out, visualizing it happening, planning for it to happen, and then take the actions necessary to make that dream on paper a reality! It's possible; many have done it before us, and many will do it after us. I have a question for you today as we close out our 90-day challenge.

What are you waiting for? Get out there and live your new life with your new mindset! I hope the 90-Day ***Mindset Challenge*** transformed your mind and life and changed how you think; we become what we think about, good or bad, so why not make it good? After all, it's our choice; it's your choice! Today I'm asking you to accept the challenges this book has given you and decide to live the life you want and never again settle for anything less than living the life of your dreams. Will it be easy? NO WAY! But will it be worth it? That answer is a ***GREAT BIG 100% YES!!!!***

I'm also hopeful that if this book helped you, you'd share it with someone you believe needs to change their mindset. It was my pleasure to share with you many of the things that have worked for me to develop my positive mindset in life. My last request to you is to PAY IT FORWARD.

Today's Challenge: Start living the life you've always dreamed of!

Positive Affirmation of the Day: I'm living the life of my dreams (Do this in the mirror)

Quote of the Day: "The only impossible journey is the one you never begin."
—Tony Robbins

Printed in Great Britain
by Amazon

37603330R00106